Ninja Foodi Digital Air Fry Oven Cookbook 2021

Amazingly Simple Air Fryer Oven Recipes to Fry, Bake, Grill, and Roast with Your Ninja Foodi Air Fry Oven| Eat Less Oil and Be Healthy| A Healthy 4-Week Meal Plan

Megan Hill

Contents

INTRODUCTION

It's a simple fact, oil is one of the indispensable ingredients in our foods. It makes sense because oil contributes to flavor and texture to our foods. Even better, oil gives cholesterol an essential substance for your body. However, cholesterol is both good and bad, depending on the amount you ingest. When taken in the right quantity it helps build healthy cells.

But, if cholesterol concentrations are too high, then it becomes a real cause for concern. In such a case, the body face the ugly face of life threatening conditions like coronary heart disease. In a bid to curtail the consumption of too much cholesterol, nutritionists ask dieter to stay away from foods with high fat or oil quantities. Out of methods advocated by nutritionists, air frying has been causing ripples in the realms of nutrition and dieting.

As a result, innovators have been in the frontline creating appliances that can aid this course. One such appliance is the Ninja Foodi Digital Airfry Oven. Even it's relatively new, the appliance has had a massive impact in the way people airfry. It's seen as a revolutionally cooking device and every household is looking to get one. If you already has the device beautifying your kitchen top, you'd want to arm yourself with plenty of recipes.

Fortunately, we've heard your cry, and gone all out to prepare a cookbook primarily for the Ninja Foodi Digital Airfry Oven. The book has 100 Ninja Foodi Digital Airfry Oven recipes, divided into different categories like Breakfast, Lunch, dinner, appetizers, poultry, and vegetarians. The best part is that all the recipes in the book use locally available ingredients and are totally easy to make.

But before you test your air frying skills, we've prepared an introduction section to help you get started with the Ninja Foodi DiGital Airfry Oven with ease. We'll let you know why the Ninja Foodi Digital Air Fry Oven is different from other air fryers and give you tips to get the best out of this amazing appliance. To make it even better, we've prepared a 4 weeks meal plan, just in case you find it hard to decide what to cook.

CHAPTER 1: Essentials of Ninja Foodi Digital Air Fryer Oven

What is Ninja Foodi Digital Air Fry Oven?

The Ninja Foodi Digital Air Fryer Oven is a convenient, one-of-a-kind cooking appliance that combines a convection oven, air fryer, and toaster oven. Put simply, the Ninja Foodi Digital air fryer is amazing kitchenware that wraps the capabilities of an Instant Pot and air fryer into a powerful all-in-one solution.

The unique kitchen appliance is easy-to-use, efficient, and versatile, and includes all the functions you could want from a multicooker. It fulfills the needs for crunchy, healthy meals, without diluting the deliciousness of the fried foods. This makes it's ideally perfect for the home cooks who marvel at diverse and delicious cooking results

While the appliance is big and doesn't spare the counter space, its unique design means you can flip the Ninja Foodi Digital Airfryer Oven up against your backsplash when it's not in use.

Features

Talking about the features, the Ninja Foodi Digital Airfryer Oven packs all the features functionality you would want in a modern cooking appliance. First, the appliance is designed to perform various functions including **air boiling, air roasting, baking, dehydrating, keeping warm, and toasting**. To cap it off, the Ninja Foodi Digital Airfryer Oven comes with a bagel function.

Second, I must say the appliance is beautifully designed and looks amazing sitting on your kitchen counter. Its color complement nearly all kitchen paintings and interior decors and will not in any way look off. Besides, the Ninja Foodi Digital Airfryer Oven is designed to flip on its back so it can be stored inconspicuously. This cool feature means that, while the appliance is overly large, when it's not in use, it will easily sit out your way.

Another interesting feature of the Ninja Foodi Digital Airfryer Oven is the control panel. This is the part that holds the operating button (START/PAUSE). Additionally, the control panel is home to all the cooking function button which are 8 in total. The best part is that all the digital controls of the Ninja Foodi Digital Airfryer Oven are easy to navigate and read. The digital display, which is usually at the top left corner, shows time and temperature readings.

Other notable features include the Preheat indicator (PRE) which flashes when the device is preheating. Besides, the appliance displays FLIP when the device is cool and can be flipped up for cleaning or storage. Most importantly, the Ninja Foodi Digital Airfryer Oven illuminates when the device is hot. This indicator turns off when the device as the cool enough and the FLIP is on.

Structural composition

The Ninja Foodi Digital Air Fryer Oven is not sophisticated when it comes to its structural composition. The cooking appliance has five main components, namely the main housing, wire rack, removable crumb tray, air fry basket, and the sheet pan.

The main housing is made of brushed stainless steel, which makes its blend in perfectly with your kitchen's interior decor. Moreover, the body is beautifully designed with the rounded corners finishing it off perfectly. Also, as mentioned earlier, the main housing accommodates the digital control pad on the left.

Besides, instead of having the towel bar handle in the front, the Foodi Digital Air Fryer Oven has a small one on the left side. Moreover, crumb-release is another pleasing feature of the device. Located at the bottom part of the ninja Foodi Digital Airfryer Oven, this feature flips down with unprecedented ease and it comes in handy when cleaning the device.

Even better, the Ninja Foodi Digital Airfryer Oven has an oven light. Putting on and off the oven is as easy as a single press of the light button on the control panel. The light allows you to check on food without opening the oven door. Lastly, the Ninja Foodi Digital Airfry Oven has a uniquely designed cord management system. The system sits at the back of the oven and doesn't interfere with the flip-away functionality.

Control panel and functions

The Ninja Foodi Digital Airfryer Oven has 8 functions:
1. **AIR FRY**: This is the function you use to make foods that were traditionally fried. It's good cooking french fries, chicken wings, and chicken nuggets without adding much oil.
2. **AIR BROIL**: best when you want to broil fish or meat.
3. **AIR ROAST**: As the name suggests, this function comes in handy when you want to roast veggies and meat. This results in foods that perfectly cooked in the inside and crispy on the outside.
4. **TOAST**: Use this function to toast bread. The size of the Ninja Foodi Digital Airfryer Oven means you can toast up to 9 slices of bread.
5. **BAKE**: Best when you want to bake homemade pizzas, cookies, and bread.
6. **BAGEL**: This is function helps toast bagel halves.
7. **DEHYDRATE**: You guessed right. The DEHYDRATE function allows you to dehydrate foods such as veggies, meat, and fruits.
8. **KEEP WARM**: As the name suggests, the function comes in handy when you cook food and want them to remain warm. Switching on this function keeps food warm for up to 2 hours.

The warranty

Initially, the Ninja Foodi Digital Airfryer Oven was only available on the Ninja store. However, following its growing demand, the appliance is now available on major e-commerce stores like Amazon and Walmart. Regardless, of where you buy your appliance, you will get a one-year limited warranty. To sweeten the deal, the Ninja Foodi Digital Airfryer Oven comes with a 60day money-back guarantee.

Benefits of using Ninja Foodi Digital Air Fry Oven?

I love delicious nuggets, tenders or good chips, everyone does. But these foods are often truncated by excess fat and oil they incorporate during cooking. Every day people are advised in hospitals or makes personal decisions to reduce the intake of the cholesterol these foods imply. One great solution is a change in the cooking method; the use of an air fryer. Let's have a quick tour of the advantages of an air fryer.

1. Prepares healthier food

An air fryer cooks with reduced or no oil unlike in deep frying where tons of oil are used. Foods with less oil are definitely healthy. It browns the food nicely and get it crispy. Foods like chicken or pork with excess oil drip it off to the air fryer drawer. Moreover, air fried food has no toxic compounds such as acrylamide which is common in deep-fried foods.

2. Quick and more efficient

Using an air fryer is faster compared to a conventional oven or stove. This is mainly because heat is concentrated in the inside and not lost to the surrounding. The air fryer also consumes minimal energy compared to other cooking appliances.

3. Safe and easy to use

Honestly, when I first bought my air fryer it was so easy to use that it made me feel like I wasn't doing things right. Some fancier modern air fryers have preset functions for specific foods. Therefore very easy to operate plus you can cook from start to finish with almost no mess to clean. Awesome right?

4. versatile

It would be easier to compile a list of what an air fryer can't do. An air fryer is one great cooking appliance that can cook almost everything. It can grill, roast, air fry, steam, bake among so many things it can do

5. Great value due to multi functions

This is one appliance with many functions. An air fryer is a fantastic solution to a household with less space. It doesn't take a lot of space and can simply be stored in a cabinet.

6. Splatter free

An air fryer is not only easy to clean but makes no mess whatsoever. The food is completely contained in the air fryer so there will no splatter, oil residue or mess on the countertop.

7. Doesn't heat up the room

Even an insulated house will heat up when an oven is cranked up for lunch or dinner. Unlike the oven, the air fryer lets out no ambient heat. The appliance may slightly be warm to touch when cooking but not to a level of heating up the room.

8. Easy to clean

By using less oil to cook, the appliance doesn't require interactive cleaning. The stainless steel finish also makes it super easy to clean.

9. Cause less odor

I know you can attest that after quick deep-frying of food, your whole house smells of fried food. The smell could even be worse if you fried fish tacos, yum. The air fryer expels steam with less fat so less odor compared to other fryers.

Did I clear your doubts about purchasing an air fryer? I am sure I did. If you love multifunctional appliances, this Ninja Foodi air fryer offers more than what you desire. An air fryer is not only an essential kitchen appliance but also an indispensable.

Why is the Ninja Foodi Digital better than the normal air fryer

I have to admit it, I'm a big fan of airfrying and have used the airfryers ever since they graced the cooking industry. Lately, Ninja introduced the Ninja Foodi Digital Airfryer Oven, a device endowed with features that make it very unique.

One, it easy to notice that this appliance is bigger than other airfryer. Its large size means the new appliance is perfect for big families that love air frying to the core. Particularly, the Ninja Foodi Digital is designed for cooking large pieces of meat and turkey.

Another thing, I found to be quite unique is that, the Ninja Foodi Digital Airfryer Oven flips on its back with ease. This means when the appliance is not in use it gets out of your way without cluttering your kitchen tops.

How to use Ninja Foodi Digital Air Fry Oven properly

Do you know how to use a Ninja Foodi digital air fryer oven? Pay keen attention to this article to help you become an expert in using this type of oven.This is the latest entry of an oven which builds off the success of already existing Ninja Foodi. It comes with a two-in-one package that is convenient which typically combines an air fryer and a toaster oven without one sacrificing the performance of the other.

As soon as it is out of its box, you get a sense of a high-quality Foodi digital air fryer oven product. It is beautifully finished with brushed stainless steel, rounded corners and a digital control pad. This digital air fryer oven is shorter and wider than typical toaster ovens.

This type of oven comes with a cooling rack, air fry basket, crumb tray, and a non-stick sheet pan.

HOW TO USE

To begin using a Ninja Foodi digital air fryer oven, simply press the power button and turn the dial to select the cooking function. Press the time-button and turn the dial to set the cooking time. Press the temp-button and turn the dial to adjust to the desired temperature. The unit will display the cooking time in hours and minutes or minutes and seconds depending on the function selected. Now press the start/pause to begin cooking.

When using toast/bake functions, press time/slice-button to select and use the dial to select the number of slices then press the temp/darkness-button and use the dial to adjust the level of darkness.

When using air/bake functions, the unit will preheat and "pre" will blink on the display. The Ninja Foodi digital air fryer oven preheats quickly so the manufacturer recommends preparing your food before starting the oven. The unit will beep once preheating is done and the timer will begin counting down from selected cook time. You can change cook time at any time by turning the dial.

The light-button helps you check on your food while cooking.

When done cooking, press the power button to turn off the oven. The hot-indicator will remain on while the oven cools off. When the oven has cooled off, the hot-indicator will turn off and "flip" will appear on the screen meaning its ready to be flipped up for storage.

How to store the Ninja Foodi digital air fryer oven

Once done cooking and the Ninja Foodi digital air fryer oven is not in use, grab the side handles and flip it up to stand at the counter back. This is a convenient and perfect storage solution.

Amazing Tips and tricks of using Ninja Foodi Digital Air Fry Oven

It's essential to research the proper use of cooking appliances every time you purchase them. When using electrical appliances, a lot of caution should be taken. Typically, the appliance always comes with an instructions manual but I felt I needed to give you a few reminders. Below are tips on using your Ninja Foodi digital air fryer.

1. Read all the instructions on the manual before installing the accessories and using the air fryer. Understand every function and hazards involved
2. Use not an extension cable. The air fryer will come with a short power supply cable that reduces the risk of people tripping or children getting entangled.
3. Do not let the air fryer cord hang over counter or table edges or touch hot surfaces. Never use the air fryer on a stovetop too..it can melt and be ruined.
4. Never cover crumb any part of the air fryer with metal foil. Covering will cause the air fryer to overheat and may even cause a fire.
5. Do not immerse power plugs and cords or the main unit in water to avoid electrical shocks.
6. Regularly inspect the air fryer power cables. if the air fryer has been damaged in any way or malfunctions, do not use it and make sure to call customer service for assistance.
7. Do not cover the air ventilation or air inlets while the air fryer is in use.do no also insert anything in the air vents. Closing them will cause overheating and may damage the unit. The unit will no longer cook.
8. Do not place heavy items on the air fryer while it's operating unless it's a recommended air fryer accessory.
9. You should ensure that all the air fryer accessories are clean and dry before placing them back to the air fryer. Other items that are not air fryer accessories shouldn't be stored in the air fryer
10. Do not use aerosol cooking spray on the inner pot of the air fryer. Trust me, its a bear to clean.
11. Install the wire rack prior to using the oven. You should also be cautious when installing any accessory in the air fryer.
12. When using the pressure cooking function on making soups, broth, or any other foods make sure you use the required amount of water for a perfect end result. This ensures that there is no contact between food and the heating element which may cause the appliance damage. Excess food load may also personal injury.

13. Do not touch the air fryer hot surfaces with bare hands during the operation and after. Ensure that you always use insulated mitts, protective hot pads, available knobs, and handles.
14. Extreme cautions should be taken when handling hot spilled food in the air fryer. Turn off the air fryer and allow it to completely cool before cleaning any spilled food and for storage. Unplug the power cable from the power source before cleaning the air fryer. Most importantly, Cleaning shouldn't be carried out by children.
15. Never unplug the power cable by grasping and pulling, carefully dry hands then unplug it from the socket.
16. Use a soft piece of cloth to clean the air fryer. Do not use metal scouring pads to clean it.
17. Last but not least your air fryer should not be used as a source of heat in the house or used for drying.

Congratulations! You are now good to go! With those tips and your air fryer instruction manual, you can safely put together your Ninja Foodi accessories and make your favorite recipes. I hope I have made you feel more confident to use your air fryer.

How to convert conventional oven recipes

Let's get one thing straight, air frying doesn't mean you frying anything, instead food in the air fryer is cooked by electric heat that is circulated by fans.the hot air keeps the food surface dry resulting in an extra crispy exterior and moist interior. Air fryers are for more than just making your favorite food in a healthy way. In fact, any food that can be roasted can be made in the air fryer. Below are some tips on how to cook your conventional oven favorite recipes in the air fryer;

1. Adjust the cooking temperatures and time

Bake your food in the air fryer at a shorter period of time but at the same conventional oven temperature. You can also bake at the same period of time but at a reduced temperature. Reduce the temperature by 25°F. The most convenient and successful method is reducing both conventional oven temperature and time. Last but not least, always remember to preheat your air fryer just as you would with a conventional oven.

2. Toss the ingredients sparingly with oil

Toss your ingredients with one or two tablespoons of oil. Oily or fattier foods need not be tossed with oil. Instead, spray the basket with cooking spray. The oil is important in getting the food more crispy and golden brown. Frozen food can be air fried without oil. A cooking spritz on them and basket won't hurt though.

3. Check for doneness early

Air circulation in the air fryer helps maintain temperature consistency unlike in a conventional oven. Therefore, foods in the air fryer tend to cook faster than in a conventional oven. You should, therefore, check your food at about two-thirds of the cooking time. Those fish sticks that are cooked in a conventional oven for 15 minutes are done in 10 minutes in an air fryer.

Are you now ready to adapt your conventional oven favorite recipes for your air fryer? I hope you are.

How to clean and maintain Ninja Foodi Digital Air Fry Oven

Like any other kitchen appliance, your air fryer should be cleaned and maintained. Failure to clean may alter its performance and accumulate flavors and odors. Your air fryer must not be immersed in water or any other cleaning liquid. You must also never clean your air fryer in a dishwasher. Here is how to clean and maintain your air fryer and keep it performing at its best.
Unplug the Device

It may sound obvious but when in a hurry, many people forget to unplug the cooking appliance from the power source. You should unplug the gadget and let it rest to cool. This helps prevent you from electrocution and injury and the air fryer is prevented from damage.

Clean the basket and pan

If your air fryer basket and the pan is dishwasher safe, just pop them in the dishwasher. If not, clean them with hot and soapy water. If the accessories have burnt or stuck food, soak them in soapy water for 10 minutes then wash off the food particles. dry the accessories before you use them again.

Clean the Interior

Use a non-abrasive sponge or a soft piece of cloth with hot water to wipe clean the heating element. Use soapy hot water to remove any grease in the interior. If there are stuck dirt particles, use a soft bristle brush to remove them. Ensure the interior has dried completely before using again

Clean the exterior

Use a soft moist sponge or cloth with a mild detergent to wipe the air fryer exterior. Do not clean the exterior using bleaches, glass cleaners or heavy cleaners. Wipe it dry after cleaning.

Keep the air fryer in peak condition

Make sure to clean your air fryer every time you use it. After proper cleaning, make sure you dry your air fryer then store it in a dry place. You can even keep in its original box but never near your dishwasher.

Never use the air fryer without the pans and basket. This is to avoid direct contact of the food and the heating element. You should also avoid overfilling the air fryer to avoid over tasking it plus the food doesn't come out as good as it should.

Small cooking appliances are often neglected. Clean them wisely and take good care of them so that they last long.

FAQs

Here are the most commonly asked questions about the Ninja Foodi Digital Airfryer Oven:

1. **What is the capacity of the Ninja Foodi Digital Air fry basket?**

The Ninja Foodi Digital Air fry basket can hold up to 4 pounds of food.

2. **Is the Ninja Foodi Digital Airfryer Oven air fryer basket nonstick?**

Unfortunately, the air fry basket is nonstick. As a result, you should the nonstick cooking spray to grease the basket when cooking food that sticks.

3. **Does the outside of the Ninja Foodi Digital Airfryer Oven get hot when air frying food?**

Yes, the outside of the device, as well as the glass window, heats up when food is cooking. However, the handle and the control panel don't heat up and always remain cool to touch.

4. **What are the time increments for the Ninja Foodi Digital Airfryer Oven?**

The Ninja Foodi Digital Airfryer Oven allows you to increase time depending on the food you are cooking. The increments vary as follows: AIR FRY (60 seconds increments up to 60 minutes), AIR BROIL (30 seconds increment up to 30 minutes), AIR ROAST (60 seconds increments up to 120 minutes), BAKE (60 seconds increment up to 120 minutes), TOAST (30seconds to 10 minutes), and KEEP WARM (5 minutes increment up to 120 minutes), and DEHYDRATE (30 minutes increment up to 12 hours)

5. What are the temperature ranges of the Ninja Foodi Digital Airfryer Oven?

The temperature ranges vary as follows, depending on the function used: AIR FRY (250°F–450°F), AIR BROIL (350°F (Lo)–450°F (Hi)), AIR ROAST (250°F–450°F), TOAST (450°F), and BAKE (250°F–400°F).

6. How much does the Ninja Foodi Digital Airfryer Oven?

The Ninja Foodi Digital Airfryer Oven price may vary depending on where you buy the device. That said, the price ranges between $239 and $269.

CHAPTER 2: 4 WEEKS MEAL PLAN

DAY	BREAKFAST	SNACK	LUNCH	DINNER
1.	Air Fryer Hard Boiled Eggs	Ninja Foodi Air Fryer Crispy Chicken Wings	Air Fryer Fish Cakes	Air fryer pork loin
2.	Air Fryer Egg Bites	Air fryer Buffalo Chicken Pull-Apart Bread	Air fryer Falafel	Air Fryer Steak
3.	Air Fryer Breakfast Stuffed Peppers	Air fryer Blooming Onion	Garlic Parmesan Air fryer French Fries	Air fryer Baked Potatoes
4.	Air fryer French Toast Sticks	Ninja Foodi and Air Fryer Bacon Wrapped Hot Dogs	Air fryer Chicken and Potatoes	Air fryer Tilapia
5.	Air Fryer Breakfast Pizza	Ninja Foodi Chocolate Oatmeal	Air Fryer Pizza	Crispy Breaded Pork Chops in the Air fryer
6.	Ninja Food French Toast Casserole	Air fryer Apple Chips	Air fryer Fajitas	Ninja Foodi Cabbage
7.	Crispy Air Fryer Potatoes	S'mores In An Air Fryer	Avocado Fries In An Air Fryer	Crispy Air-fried Tofu
8.	Air fryer Breakfast Frittata	Mexican Air Fryer Corn on the Cob	Rotisserie-Style Chicken In An Air Fryer	Air fryer pork loin
9.	Easy Air Fryer Donut	Air Fryer Sweet Potato Tots	Air Fryer Meatloaf	Air fryer Rotisserie Chicken
10	Air Fryer Bagels	Air Fryer Doughnuts	Mexican - style Air Fryer Stuffed Chicken Breasts	Air Fryer Cheesy Beef Enchiladas
11	Air Fryer Cinnamon Rolls	Air Fryer Banana Bread	Air Fryer Herb and Cheese-Stuffed Burgers	Air Fryer Scallops
12	Ninja Foodi Breakfast Omelette	Air-fried Butter Cake	Air Fryer Chick-Fil-A Chicken Sandwich	Air Fryer Southern Style Catfish With Green Beans
13	Ninja Food French Toast Casserole	Air Fryer Doughnuts	Air Fryer Roast Beef	Air Fryer Salmon with Horseradish Rub
14	Air Fryer Egg Bites	Air Fryer Tuna Patties	Ninja Foodi French Fries	Air fryer Rotisserie Chicken
15	Easy Air Fryer Donut	Ninja Foodi and Air Fryer Bacon	Air Fryer Beef Kabobs	Air fryer Salmon Cake

		Wrapped Hot Dogs		
16	Air Fryer Hard Boiled Eggs	Air fryer Apple Chips	Garlic Parmesan Air fryer French Fries	Crispy Breaded Pork Chops in the Air fryer
17	Air Fryer Breakfast Pizza	Air Fryer Chicken Nuggets	Ninja Foodi Air Fryer Cauliflower	Air Fryer Everything Bagel Chicken roll-ups
18	Air fryer French Toast Sticks	Ninja Foodi Zucchini Chips	Ninja Foodi Brussels Sprout	Air Fryer Mongolian Beef
19	Ninja Food French Toast Casserole	Air-fryer Fish Sticks	Air fried General Tso's Chicken	Air fryer Garlic Rosemary Brussels Sprouts
20	Air fryer Breakfast Frittata	Ninja Foodi Air Fryer Crispy Chicken Wings	Air Fryer Lemon Pepper Shrimp	Ninja Foodi Sweet Potato
21	Ninja Foodi Breakfast Omelet	Air fryer Blooming Onion	Air fryer Falafel	Cauliflower Taco Bowl
22	Air Fryer Cinnamon Rolls	Mexican Air Fryer Corn on the Cob	Spicy Lamb Sirloin Steak	Air Fryer Korean BBQ Beef
23	Air Fryer Bagels	Air-Fried Chickpeas	Air Fryer Baked Russet Potatoes	Crispy Veggie Quesadillas in an Air Fryer
24	Easy Air Fryer Donut	Air Fryer Sweet Potato Tots	Air Fryer Orange Beef	Air Fryer Cheesy Beef Enchiladas
25	Crispy Air Fryer Potatoes	Air Fryer Chicken Nuggets	Mexican - style Air Fryer Stuffed Chicken Breasts	Air Fryer Beef And Broccoli
26	Air Fryer Breakfast Pizza	Air-Fryer Spinach Artichoke Dip	Air-Fried Parmesan Mushrooms	Air Fryer Southern Style Catfish With Green Beans
27	Air Fryer Breakfast Stuffed Peppers	Ninja Foodi Chocolate Oatmeal	Air Fryer Rib Eye Steak With Blue Cheese Butter	Air Fryer Spicy Green Beans
28	Air Fryer Egg Bites	Air Fryer Tuna Patties	Air Fryer Roasted Okra	Air Fryer Scallops

CHAPTER 3: NINJA FOODI DIGITAL AIR FRY OVEN RECIPES

DELICIOUS BREAKFAST

Air Fryer Hard Boiled Eggs

Who doesn't love boiled eggs? Hard-boiled eggs are great in high protein snack, potato salad and above all a great breakfast.whether you love soft boiled eggs or hard-boiled eggs, the air fryer has got you covered.

Prep time: 5 minutes, **Cook time**: 14 minutes; **Serves**:6

Ingredients

6 eggs

Preparation Method

1. Place the eggs in an air fryer without overlapping them.
2. Turn the air fryer on and close the lid. Set to 270°F for 10 minutes for a runny yolk,14 minutes for a soft yolk, and 15 for a hard yolk.
3. When the time has elapsed, transfer the eggs to a bowl with ice-cold water.
4. Remove shells once cold. Serve and enjoy

Nutritional Information

Calories 62, Total Fat 4g, Saturated Fat 1g, Total Carbs 0g, Net Carbs 0g, Protein 5g, Sugar 0g, Fiber 0g, Sodium 62mg, Potassium 60mg

Air Fryer Egg Bites

I love Starbucks egg bites, in fact, I love them loaded with a lot of bacon. I bet everybody does. The good news is, you can now make them right at your home, in your air fryer. Just 10 minutes, and your breakfast or snack will be ready.

Prep time:10 minutes, **Cook time**: 10 minutes; **Serves**: 4

Ingredients

4 eggs

4 tbsp milk

½ onion, diced

½ green bell pepper, diced

4 strips bacon, cooked and crumbled

¼ cup cheese, shredded

Salt and pepper to taste

Preparation Method

1. Arrange four silicon cupcake holders in the air fryer basket.
2. Crack an egg and add 1 tablespoon of milk to each cupcake holder.
3. Top each with some onions, pepper, bacon, and cheese.
4. Sprinkle each with salt and pepper.
5. Air fry for 10 13 minutes at 300°F or until golden brown.
6. Serve and enjoy.

Nutritional Information

Calories 195, Total Fat 15g, Saturated Fat 6g, Total Carbs 3g, Net Carbs 2g, Protein 10g, Sugar 1g, Fiber 1g, Sodium 255mg, Potassium 144mg

Air Fryer Breakfast Stuffed Peppers

 If starting on a keto diet, you know eggs are a big yes. These stuffed bell peppers can spice things a little bit. They are however not only for those on a low carb diet but for everyone. These stuffed bell peppers are healthy, high in protein and simply the best breakfast to kick off your day with.

Prep time: 5 minutes, **Cook time**: 13 minutes; **Serves**: 2

Ingredients

1 tbsp olive oil

1 bell pepper, halved and seed removed

4 eggs

1 tbsp olive oil

1 pinch salt and pepper

1 pinch sriracha flakes

Preparation Method

1. Rub olive oil on the peppers exposed edges.
2. Crack an egg on each pepper half and sprinkle your desired spices.
3. Set the pepper halves on a trivet in the air fryer and close the lid.
4. Air fry at 390◦C for 13 minutes or at 330◦F for 15 minutes for a hard egg.
5. Serve and enjoy.

Nutritional Information

Calories 164, Total Fat 10g, Saturated Fat 3g, Total Carbs 4g, Net Carbs 3g, Protein 11g, Sugar 2g, Fiber 1g, Sodium 146g, Potassium 246g

Air fryer French Toast Sticks

My mornings are just hectic even without the school being in session so I look for easy meal solutions. These French toast sticks are quick, easy to make and are perfect for those busy mornings. You can make them ahead of time, freeze them in a single layer on a lined parchment baking sheet and just reheat in the morning.

Prep time: 7 minutes, **Cook time**: 8 minutes; **Serves**: 12

Ingredients

12 slices Texas Toast

1 cup milk

5 large eggs

4 tbsp butter, melted

1 tbsp vanilla extract

¼ cup granulated sugar

1 tbsp cinnamon

Maple syrup

Preparation Method

1. Slice the bread slices into thirds.
2. Whisk together milk, eggs, butter, and vanilla in a mixing bowl until well combined.
3. In a separate bowl, mix sugar and cinnamon.
4. Dip each breadstick in the egg mixture then sprinkle the sugar mixture on both sides.
5. Place the sticks in an air fryer basket and cook at 350°F for 8 minutes.
6. Transfer from the basket to a platter and allow to cool. Serve with maple syrup and enjoy.

Nutritional Information

Calories 170, Total Fat 8g, Saturated Fat 4g, Total Carbs 19g, Net Carbs 18g, Protein 6g, Sugar 7g, Fiber 1g, Sodium 183mg

Air Fryer Breakfast Pizza

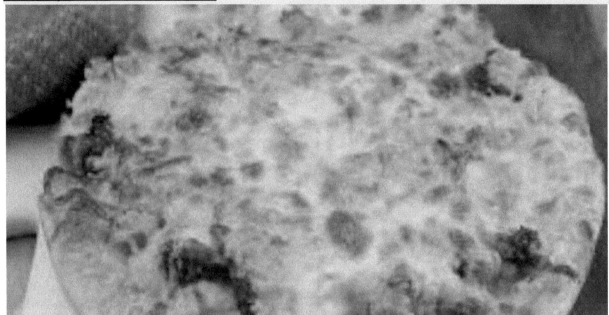

A light, tender but flaky crust loaded with eggs, cheese and sausage is all you and your family needs for breakfast. It's crazy easy to throw together and the air fryer gives the crust a golden brown texture.

Prep time: 5 minutes, **Cook time**: 20 minutes; **Serves**: 4

Ingredients

Crescent dough

3 scrambled eggs

Crumbled sausage

½ pepper, chopped

½ cup cheddar cheese

½ cup mozzarella cheese

Preparation Method

1. Spray a springform pan with oil then spread the dough at the bottom.
2. Place the pan in an air fryer at 350ᵒF for 5 minutes or until browned slightly.
3. Top with eggs, sausage, chopped peppers, and cheese.
4. Return to the air fryer for 10 minutes or until golden brown.
5. Slice the pizza and enjoy.

Nutritional Information

Calories 250, Total Fat 19g, Saturated Fat 9g, Total Carbs 5g, Net Carbs 5g, Protein 14g, Sugar 2g, Fiber 0g, Sodium 424mg

Ninja Food French Toast Casserole

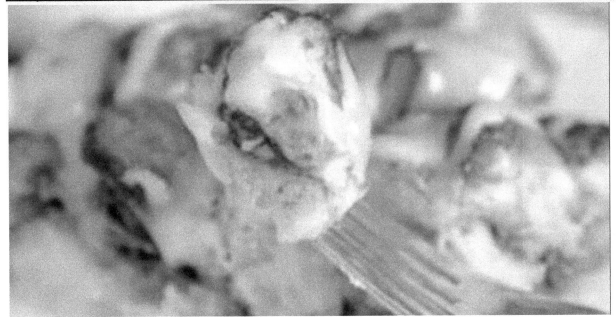

 Are you looking for an awesome breakfast to serve on Christmas, birthdays, Valentine's day mornings? A light and moist toast casserole with a vanilla hint and paired with salty bacon is the tastiest breakfast you can ever come around. Try this toast casserole in your air fryer and I know you will love its simplicity.

Prep time: 5 minutes, **Cook time**: 20minutes; **Serves**: 6

Ingredients

4 eggs

1 tbsp vanilla

2 tbsp milk

2 packs Grands Cinnamon rolls

Preparation Method

1. Whisk together eggs, vanilla, and milk in a mixing bowl.
2. Open the cinnamon rolls then quarter each dough reserving the icing.
3. Spray the ninja food insert with cooking oil.
4. Place dough in a pan then pour over egg mixture.
5. Close the lid and at 350°F for 20 minutes.
6. Top with reserved icing or with syrup

Nutritional Information

Calories 161, Total Fat 6g, Saturated Fat 2g, Total Carbs 20g, Net Carbs 19g, Protein 6g, Sugar 8g, Fiber 1g, Sodium 229

Crispy Air Fryer Potatoes

Air fryer gives your potatoes a crispy texture making them perfect for breakfast. They are simple to make; just 20 minutes and your breakfast is ready. You can carry the leftovers to work in your lunchbox.

Prep time: 5 minutes, **Cook time**: 20 minutes; **Serves**: 8

Ingredients

1 ½ lb Golden potatoes, diced into ½ inch thick cubes

1 tbsp avocado oil

1 tbsp garlic powder

1 tbsp paprika

2 tbsp salt

1 tbsp ground black pepper

Preparation Method

1. Toss the potatoes with avocado oil, garlic powder, paprika, salt, and pepper until well coated.
2. Place the potatoes in an air fryer basket and set at 400°F for 20 minutes.
3. When halfway through the cooking cycle, toss the potatoes so they cook evenly.
4. Remove the potatoes from the air fryer and serve. Enjoy

Nutritional Information

Calories 68, Total Fat 1g, Saturated Fat 0g, Total Carbs 10g, Net Carbs 10g, Protein 0g, Sugar 1g

Air fryer Breakfast Frittata

Nothing is easy like making a frittata in a cake pan fitted in an air fryer basket. Switch up ingredients as you desire to suit your taste. This frittata will definitely help you win over your kids and spouse.

Prep time: minutes, **Cook time**: minutes; **Serves**:

Ingredients

¼ lb breakfast sausage, cooked and crumbled

4 eggs, beaten lightly

½ cup Cheddar Monterey jack cheese blend, shredded

2 tbsp red bell pepper, diced

1 green onion, chopped

1 pinch cayenne pepper

Cooking spray

Preparation Method

1. Combine all ingredients except cooking spray in a mixing bowl.
2. Preheat your air fryer to 360°F and spray cooking spray on a 6x2 inch cake pan.
3. Pour the egg mixture in the cake pan.
4. Place the lid and cook for 18 20 minutes or until the frittata is set.
5. Slice and serve. Enjoy.

Nutritional Information

Calories 380, Total Fat 27.4g, Saturated Fat 12g, Total Carbs 2.9g, Net Carbs 2.5, Protein 31.2, Sugar 1g, Fiber 0.4g, Sodium 694mg, Potassium 328mg

Easy Air Fryer Donut

Are you ready for comfort food in a single bite? The donut is one of the best air fryer recipes around as when covered with sugar and cinnamon and a frosting drizzle on top, it makes a great breakfast.

Prep time: 10 minutes, **Cook time:** 6 minutes; **Serves** 6

Ingredients

1 roll cinnamon rolls, refrigerated and cut in half

2 tbsp melted butter

¼ cup cinnamon

½ cup sugar

Preparation Method

1. Preheat your air fryer to 390◦F.
2. Meanwhile, roll the refrigerated cinnamon rolls into balls. Each into a ball, tight.
3. Place butter in a bowl, small, then pour sugar and cinnamon into a baggie, pint-size. Shake well to mix. Dip each cinnamon ball into butter until completely coated then transfer into the pint-sized baggie shaking to coat outside with sugar and cinnamon.
4. In the meantime, prepare your air fryer basket by spraying with no-stick spray.
5. Place coated cinnamon balls into the basket. Space them for balls will spread. 8 pieces at a time. Close the air fryer and air fry them for about 5-6 minutes at 390◦F. Check if it's done through at 5 minutes mark.
6. Place the remaining cinnamon and sugar in a new pint-sized baggie then recoat each donut with more cinnamon and sugar. Each at a time.
7. Drizzle each with frosting from the cinnamon roll container.Serve and enjoy.

Nutritional Information

Calories: 312, Total Fat: 13g, Saturated Fat: 6g, Total Carbs: 47g, Net Carbs: 46g, Protein: 3g, Sugars: 30g, Fiber: 1g, Sodium: 474mg, Potassium: 673mg

Air Fryer Bagels

These bagels are delicious and easy when made in a Ninja Foodi. They emerge crispy having a soft-chewy center. You will love and enjoy them.

Prep time: 15 minutes, **Cook time:** 9 minutes; **Serves**

Ingredients

1 cup flour, self-rising

1 cup Greek yogurt

Optional: ½ cup whipped cream cheese

Optional: 2 tbsp sugar and cinnamon

Preparation Method

1. Mix together yogurt and flour until dough consistency forms. Form equal-sized balls from the dough.Meanwhile, spray a springform pan inside using non-stick spray or line trivet with parchment paper.
2. Place the balls into the pan making sure there is space between them. 7 balls at a time.
3. If desired, Splash equally with a mixture of sugar and cinnamon.
4. Close the air fryer and air fry them for about 5 minutes at 325∘F for bagel bites. 9 minutes for whole bagels.
5. Open the fryer and flip. Splash again with sugar and cinnamon if desired.
6. Set again at 325∘F for about 4 minutes for bagel bites or 6 minutes for whole bagels.
7. Remove and set aside to completely cool then fill with cream cheese after making a hole on the side using a knife, small. Enjoy!

Nutritional Information

Calories: 957, Total Fat: 41g, Saturated Fat: 22g, Total Carbs: 102mg, Net Carbs: 99g, Protein: 42g, Sugar: 10g, Fiber: 3g, Sodium: 438mg, Potassium: 563mg

Air Fryer Cinnamon Rolls

If you are obsessed with making air fryer recipes, try this one. They are the best cinnamon rolls ever made in an air fryer. They are made with no yeast and only requires 20 minutes to be ready.

Prep time: 10 minutes, **Cook time:** 10 minutes; **Serves** 10

Ingredients

1 roll refrigerated crescent rolls

⅓ cup brown sugar

⅓ cup melted butter

¼ cup raisins

⅓ cup chopped nuts, walnuts or pecans

2 tbsp maple syrup

2 tbsp sugar

1 tbsp cinnamon

Preparation Method

1. Whisk together sugar, butter, and maple syrup in a medium bowl.
2. In the meantime, place a trivet into your Ninja Foodi/air fryer inside and 8-inch springform pan after spraying the top with non-stick spray.
3. Pour the sugar mixture into the pan then splash with raisins and nuts.
4. Open the crescent rolls package and place the crescent roll on a board, cutting. Do not unroll but cut to half using a knife, non-serrated one. Cut the pieces equally until 8 equal pieces.
5. Mix sugar and cinnamon in a small bowl then dip the top and bottom of each piece into the mixture. Place the pieces over the sugar mixture in the pan.
6. Cover the air fryer and air fry for about 5 minutes at 345◦F. Open your air fryer and flip each piece. Cover again and air fry for another 4 minutes at 345◦F.
7. Remove pan and place the buns on a serving plate. Scoop the mixture at the pan bottom over the rolls. Enjoy!

Nutritional Information

Calories: 143, Total Fat: 8g, Saturated Fat: 4g, Total Carbs: 17g, Net Carbs: 16g, Protein: 1g, Sugar: 11g, Fiber: 1g, Sodium: 58mg, Potassium: 77mg

Ninja Foodi Breakfast Omelette

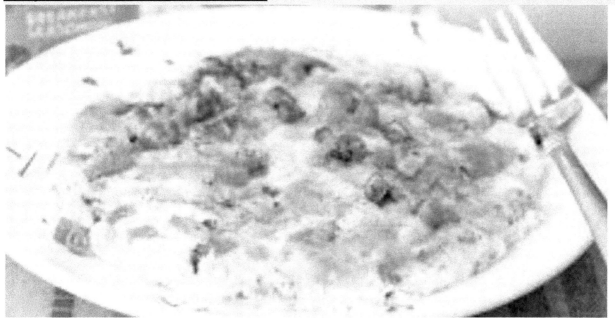

This will become your favorite breakfast omelet made in an air fryer. The omelet is filled with cheese, eggs, and ground bacon or sausage. Everyone will absolutely love it.

Prep time: 10 minutes, **Cook time**: 11 minutes; **Serves** 6

Ingredients

¾ cup diced onion

1 tbsp olive oil

5 sliced mushrooms

8 scrambled eggs

¼ cup mushroom soup cream

½ tbsp garlic salt

¾ cup shredded cheese

½ lb ground sausage, spicy

Optional: 1 diced chives

Preparation Method

1. Turn on your Ninja Foodi to saute setting then add olive oil, onions, and sausage/bacon.
2. Cook until done halfway then add mushrooms. Cook until no pink is seen then press stop.
3. Pour scrambled eggs over meat in the Ninja Foodi then splash with mushroom soup cream, garlic salt, and ½ cup cheese. Stir to combine.
4. Close your air fryer and air fry for about 6 minutes at 390◦F.
5. Open and stir for the uncooked egg at the bottom to circulate and to cook through..
6. Cover and air fry for an additional 4-5 minutes at 390◦F or until desired consistency.
7. Splash with chives and serve with remaining cheese. Enjoy!

Nutritional Information

Calories: 294, Total Fat: 22g, Saturated Fat: 8g, Total Carbs: 3g, Net Carbs: 2g, Protein: 17g, Sugar: 1g, Fiber: 1g, Sodium: 681mg, Potassium: 283mg

Air Fryer Fish Cakes

If you are a fish lover then these easy and quick to make fish sticks will be a great in your lunch box or just a home lunch. The Thai chili sauce, cilantro, and a lemon squeeze give these patties an irresistible taste that will win over every member of your family.

Prep time: 10 minutes, **Cook time**: 10 minutes; **Serves**: 2

Ingredients

Cooking spray

10 oz white fish, finely chopped

⅔ cup panko breadcrumbs, whole wheat

3 tbsp cilantro, freshly chopped

2 tbsp Thai sweet chili sauce

2 tbsp canola mayonnaise

1 egg

⅛ tbsp salt

¼ tbsp ground pepper

2 lime wedges

Preparation Method

1. Coat the air fryer basket with cooking spray.
2. In a mixing bowl, combine all the ingredients except lemon wedges until well combined. Now shape the fish mixture into 4 3" diameter cakes.
3. Coat the prepared cakes with cooking spray and arrange them in the air fryer basket.
4. Cook at 400°F for 10 minutes or until the cakes are browned.
5. When the time has elapsed, squeeze the lime over the cakes and serve. Enjoy

Nutritional Information

Calories 399, Total Fat 15.5g, Saturated Fat 2.1g, Total Carbs 27.9g, Net Carbs 25.1g, Protein 34.6g, Sugar 10g, Fiber 2.8g, Sodium 537mg, Potassium 731mg

Air fryer Falafel

Unlike pan-fried falafels, Air fryer falafels are crisper and with less oil. Falafels are also easy to cook; you just need to combine all the ingredients in your blender, make patties and drop them in the air fryer basket. Serve these falafels with tahini sauce for a comforting and filling lunch.

Prep time: 25 minutes, **Cook time**: 20 minutes; **Serves**: 4

Ingredients

1 cup dry chickpeas soak overnight

½ cup flat-leaf parsley, freshly packed

¼ cup onion, chopped

2 garlic cloves

1 tbsp extra virgin oil

1 tbsp lemon juice

1 tbsp cumin, ground

½ tbsp salt

¼ tbsp baking soda

1-3tbsp water

Preparation Method

1. Drain the chickpeas then add all the ingredients to the food processor. Pulse while adding water if required.
2. Use 3 tablespoons of the mixture to make 12 1 ½ inch patties.
3. Lightly coat the air fryer basket with cooking spray then arrange the patties in a single layer. Coat the patties top with more cooking spray.
4. Cook at 375°F for 20 minutes turning the patties halfway through the cooking time.
5. Serve the patties with tahini sauce for dipping and enjoy.

Nutritional Information

Calories 216, Total Fat 6.5g, Saturated Fat 0.8g, Total Carbs 31g, Net Carbs22.2g, Protein 9.8g, Sugar 6g, Fiber 8.8g, Sodium 384mg, Potassium 367mg

Garlic Parmesan Air fryer French Fries

 I think everyone knows that fries are classic comfort food epitome. I also think fries are almost everyone's favorite. Making these french fries at home is better than grabbing frozen ones from the stores. The air fryer will make your french fries without compromising neither comfort, flavor nor your health.

Prep time: 20 minutes, **Cook time**: 20 minutes; **Serves**: 1

Ingredients

2 russet potatoes, cut into thin wedges

1 tbsp olive oil

1 tbsp granulated garlic

¼ cup parmesan cheese, grated

¼ tbsp salt

¼ tbsp black pepper, ground

1 tbsp fresh parsley, finely chopped

Preparation Method

1. Preheat your air fryer to 400⁰F.
2. Put the potatoes in a mixing bowl then drizzle olive oil. Toss the potatoes to coat.
3. Sprinkle garlic, cheese, salt, and pepper then transfer the potatoes to the air fryer basket.
4. Air fry for 20 minutes or until golden brown and crispy. Ensure you stir halfway the cooking time. Top with parsley and serve when warm with classic ketchup. Enjoy

Nutritional Information

Calories 37, Total Fat 1g, Saturated Fat 0g, Total Carbs 5g, Net Carbs 4g, Protein 1g, Sugar 0g, Fiber 1g, Sodium 65mg

Air fryer Chicken and Potatoes

No more eating dry chicken friends. The air fryer makes you a gorgeous chicken that has a dark color on the outside but juicy on the inside. This crispy super easy herbed chicken lunch is a winner.

Prep time: 5 minutes, **Cook time**: 25 minutes; **Serves**: 6

Ingredients

½ tbsp sea salt

½ tbsp garlic powder

½ tbsp herbes de Provence

½ tbsp onion, dried and minced

¼ tbsp black pepper, ground

3 chicken breasts, boneless and skinless

1 lb baby potatoes

Olive oil spray

Broccoli florets

Preparation Method

1. In a mixing bowl, mix salt, garlic, herbes de Provence, onions, and black pepper.
2. Place the chicken and potatoes on the air fryer cooking tray then spritz with cooking oil.
3. Season the chicken and potatoes with the garlic mixture then spritz the chicken with oil.
4. Preheat air fryer to 390°F then add the chicken and potatoes to the air fryer. Cook for 25 minutes rotating the cooking tray halfway the cooking time.
5. Add broccoli during the last 5 minutes of cooking time.
6. Serve and enjoy.

Nutritional Information

Calories 125, Total Fat 2g, Saturated Fat 1g, Total Carbs 14g, Net Carbs 12g, Protein 14g, Sugar 1g, Fiber 2g, Sodium 264mg, Potassium 534mg

Air Fryer Pizza

This will probably become your kid's favorite meal. The air fryer pizza is easy and super quick as it takes less than 20 minutes to make. Great for main dish especially lunch.

Prep time: 10 minutes, **Cook time**: 10 minutes; **Serves:** 2

Ingredients

1 package, 6.5 -z, pizza dough mix

¼ cup spaghetti sauce

½ - ¾ cup mozzarella cheese

Optional: pepperoni

Optional: olives

Olive oil spray

Preparation Method

1. Preheat an air fryer for about 3 minutes at 320°F.
2. Make pizza dough.
3. Meanwhile, spray a 7-inch springform pan with olive oil spray then spread the dough across the pan. Make sure it's level.
4. Place the pan into an air fryer then spray pizza dough top with olive oil spray.
5. Close the air fryer and set for about 3 minutes at 320°F for dough to cook a bit.
6. Open then add cheese, spaghetti sauce, pepperoni, and other toppings.
7. Close and set against for about 7 minutes at 320°F.
8. Serve and enjoy.

Nutritional Information

Calories: 454, Total Fat: 13g, Saturated Fat: 6g, Total Carbs: 70g, Net Carbs: 67g, Protein: 15g, Sugar: 6g, Fiber: 3g, Sodium: 1321mg, Potassium: 303mg

Air fryer Fajitas

Do you love Fajitas? This is an amazing lunch recipe for you. Making air fryer fajitas is easy and everyone will love as skirt steak has more flavor than flank.

Prep time: 15 minutes, **Cook time**: 8 minutes; **Serves** 4

Ingredients

1 lb sliced skirt steak

2 sliced bell peppers

½ sliced onion, large

3 tbsp olive oil

½ tbsp chili powder

¼ tbsp pepper

1½ tbsp cumin

1 tbsp salt

1 tbsp garlic powder

½ tbsp dry sriracha

Preparation Method

1. Place steak into a medium bowl then pour 2 tbsp olive oil over. Mix together.
2. Combine your spices into a small bowl and mix them together.
3. Add meat to the spices mixture then stir to coat.
4. Add onions, bell peppers, and 1 tbsp olive oil. Stir for meat and vegetables to be coated well.
5. Preheat an air fryer for about 3 minutes at 390°F.
6. Place half of the fajita mixture into the air fryer basket spreading out for a little overlap.
7. Close and air fry for about 7 minutes at 320°F or until done. Stir at 5 minutes mark.
8. Repeat for the remaining fajita mixture.
9. Serve inside tortillas, small, then top with avocado, sour cream etc..Enjoy!

Nutritional Information

Calories: 417, Total fat: 34g, Saturated fat: 10g, Total carbs: 7g, Net carbs: 5g, Protein: 21g, Sugar: 3g, Fiber: 2g, Sodium: 679mg, Potassium: 514mg

Avocado Fries In An Air Fryer

Oh yes! Avocado fries are next-level darned good for it is creamy and crunchy making this recipe irresistible and an ultimate fryer indulgence.

Prep time: 15 minutes, **Cook time**: 15 minutes; **Serves** 4

Ingredients

½ cup all-purpose flour

1½ tbsp black pepper

2 eggs, large

1 tbsp water

½ tbsp panko, Japanese-style Breadcrumbs

2 avocados, each cut to 8 wedges

Cooking spray

¼ tbsp kosher salt

¼ cup ketchup, no-salt-added

2 tbsp canola mayonnaise

1 tbsp apple cider vinegar

1 tbsp sriracha chili sauce

Preparation Method

1. Stir together pepper and flour in a dish, shallow. Beat eggs lightly and water in another dish, shallow. Place panko in another shallow dish. Dredge flour mixture into avocado then shake off excess. Pour in egg mixture and allow excess to fall.Dredge in panko then press to adhere.
2. Coat with cooking spray then place the wedges into your air fryer basket.
3. Cook for about 7-8 minutes at 400°F until golden. Turn halfway through.
4. Remove from the air fryer then sprinkle with salt.
5. Meanwhile, whisk together, mayonnaise, ketchup, sriracha, and vinegar in a bowl, small, until combined into a sauce. Divide avocado fries among 2 plates then scoop 2tbsp sauce into each plate. Enjoy!

Nutritional Information

Calories: 262, Total Fat:18g Saturated Fat: 3g, Total Carbs: 23g, Net Carbs: 16g, Protein: 5g, Sugar: 5g, Fiber: 7g, Sodium: 306mg, Potassium: 421mg

Rotisserie-Style Chicken In An Air Fryer

This recipe is easy and will make new air fryer users feel pro. The recipe is amazing and makes a great lunch dish.

Prep time: 10 minutes, **Cook time**: 1 hour; **Serves** 6

Ingredients

1 whole chicken, rinsed and any items removed from the inside bird

2½ tbsp garlic salt

½ tbsp pepper

1 tbsp onion powder

½ tbsp seasoned salt

½ tbsp oregano

3 tbsp olive oil

Preparation Method

1. Dry the chicken with paper towels then rub the outside skin with olive oil.
2. Place the chicken in an air fryer basket with breast-side down.
3. Splash half of the seasonings over chicken then close your air fryer.
4. Air fry for about 30 minutes at 360°F.
5. Open the fryer, flip the chicken, then spray with olive oil spray and splash with remaining seasonings.
6. Close the fryer and set for another 30 minutes at 360°F or until cooked through.
7. Serve and enjoy.

Nutritional Information

Calories: 337, Total fat: 26g, Saturated fat: 6g, Total carbs: 1g, Net carbs: 0g, Protein: 24g, Sugar: 1g, Fiber: 1g, Sodium: 3190mg, Potassium: 240mg

Air Fryer Meatloaf

This recipe is simple to prepare in under 1 hour. When prepared in an air fryer, the meatloaf comes out greatly that everyone including your kids will love.

Prep time: 10 minutes, **Cook time**: 25 minutes; **Serves** 4

Ingredients

1 lb lean beef, ground

1 lightly beaten egg

3 tbsp bread crumbs, dry

1 finely chopped onion, small

1 tbsp fresh thyme, chopped

1 tbsp salt

Ground black pepper to taste

2 thinly sliced mushrooms

1 tbsp olive oil

Preparation Method

1. Preheat your air fryer to 200∘C or 392∘F.
2. In the meantime, combine beef, bread crumbs, egg, thyme, onion, pepper, and salt in a medium bowl. Knead with your hands to mix thoroughly.
3. Transfer the mixture into a baking pan then smoothen the top.
4. Press mushrooms to the top then use olive oil to coat.
5. Place the baking pan into the fryer basket.
6. Cover your air fryer and set for about 25 minutes roasting until meatloaf is browned nicely.
7. Now let the meatloaf rest for about 10 minutes, then slice into wedges.
8. Serve and enjoy.

Nutritional Information

Calories: 297, Total Fat: 18.8g, Saturated Fat: 6g, Total Carbs: 5.9g, Net Carbs: 5.1g, Protein: 24.8g, Sugar: 1g, Fiber: 0.8g, Sodium: 706mg, Potassium: 361mg

Mexican - style Air Fryer Stuffed Chicken Breasts

Just above 10 minutes in the fryer comes out a tender and juicy chicken breasts. The recipe is quick, easy, and perfect when served with tortillas and pico de gallo.

Prep time: 20 minutes, **Cook time**: 10 minutes; **Serves** 2

Ingredients

4 toothpicks, extra-long

4 tbsp divided chili powder

4 tbsp divided ground cumin

1 chicken breast, boneless and skinless

2 tbsp chipotle flakes

2 tbsp Mexican oregano

Ground black pepper and salt to taste

½ sliced red bell pepper, thin strips

1 sliced fresh jalapeno pepper, thin strips

2 tbsp corn oil

½ juiced lime

Preparation Method

1. Place extra-long toothpicks in a bowl, small, then cover them with water. Soak them to prevent burning when cooking.
2. Mix 2tbsp cumin and 2 tbsp chili powder in a dish, shallow one.
3. In the meantime, preheat your air fryer to 200◦c or 400◦F.
4. Slice the chicken horizontally placed on a flat surface then pound the halves with a rolling pin or kitchen mallet until ¼ - inch thick.
5. Equally splash each breast half with 2tbsp cumin, 2tbsp chili powder, chipotle flakes, pepper, salt, and oregano.
6. Place onion, ½ bell pepper, and jalapeno in the breast half center then roll the breast half and secure with 2 toothpicks. Roll from tapered end upward.
7. Repeat for the other breast half with vegetables and spices then secure with 2 toothpicks.

8. Roll each rolled breast half into chili-cumin mixture. Drizzle with olive oil while rolling until covered evenly.
9. Place the rolled breast halves into a fryer basket with toothpick facing up.
10. Cook for about 6 minutes then turn over the roll-ups.
11. Continue to cook for an additional 5 minutes until a thermometer, instant-read, register 165°F or 74°C.
12. Drizzle each roll-up with lime juice.
13. Serve and enjoy.

Nutritional Information

Calories: 185, Total Fat: 8.5g, Saturated fat: 1.3g, Total carbs: 15.2g, Net carbs: 9.8g, Protein: 14.8g, Sugar: 5g, Fiber: 5.4g, Sodium: 171mg, Potassium: 499mg

Air Fryer Herb and Cheese-Stuffed Burgers

Do you want to wake up taste buds? Try this recipe for they are quick hamburgers made in the air fryer with a creamy cheese filling. It is also perfect for people tired of old beef burgers.

Prep time: 20 minutes, **Cook time**: 15 minutes, **Serves** 4

Ingredients

2 green thinly sliced onions

2 tbsp fresh parsley, minced

4 tbsp divided Dijon Mustard

3 tbsp bread crumbs, dry

2 tbsp ketchup

½ tsp salt

½ tbsp dried and crushed rosemary

¼ tbsp sage leaves, dried

1 lb lean ground beef

2 oz sliced cheddar cheese

4 hamburger buns

Optional toppings: lettuce leaves, mayonnaise, sliced tomato, and additional ketchup.

Preparation Method

1. Preheat your air fryer to 375◦F.
2. Combine green onions, 2 tbsp mustard, and parsley in a bowl, small.
3. Mix bread crumbs, seasonings, ketchup, and 2 tbsp mustard in another small bowl.
4. Add beef to the crumb mixture then lightly mix but thoroughly. Shape mixture into 8 patties, thin. Place cheese between 4 patties then spoon onion mixture over cheese and top with other 4 patties. Press edges firmly together to completely seal.
5. Place the burgers in a fryer basket in one layer. If needed, work in batches.
6. Close and air fry for about 8 minutes.Flip and cook for another 6-8 minutes until 160◦F is registered on a thermometer. Top with any optional toppings if desired. Serve and enjoy!

Nutritional Information

Calories: 369, Total Fat: 14g, Saturated Fat: 6g, Total Carbs: 29g, Net Carbs: 28g, Protein: 29g, Sugar: 6g, Fiber: 1g, Sodium: 850mg, Potassium: 679mg

Air Fryer Chick-Fil-A Chicken Sandwich

You don't have to visit a restaurant, this chicken sandwich is homemade and perfect for any weekday or on Sundays. It is a lunch dish that is amazing and you will enjoy making it.

Prep time: 10 minutes, **Cook time**: 16 minutes; **Serves** 6

Ingredients

2 pounded skinless chicken breast, boneless

½ cup dill Pickle Juice

2 eggs

½ cup milk

1 cup all-purpose flour

2 tbsp powdered sugar

2 tbsp potato starch

1 tbsp paprika

1 tbsp sea salt

½ tbsp black pepper, freshly ground

½ tbsp garlic powder

¼ tbsp celery seed, ground

1 tbsp olive oil, extra-virgin

4 toasted hamburger buns

8 dill pickle chips

Optional spicy: ¼ tbsp cayenne pepper

Preparation Method

1. Make sure the pounded chicken is ½-inch thick.
2. Cut the breasts into 2-3 pieces making sure each piece is bigger than buns.
3. Place the pieces into a Ziploc baggie then pour pickle juice in. place in the refrigerator for about 30 minutes to marinate the chicken.
4. Beat eggs with milk in a bowl, medium.
5. Combine flour, all spices and starch in another medium bowl.
6. Use tongs to coat the chicken pieces in the egg mixture then in the flour mixture. Make sure chicken pieces are coated completely shaking off excess flour.

7. Spray your fryer basket with oil then place chicken pieces. Spray the pieces with oil.
8. Cook for about 6 minutes at 340◦F.
9. Flip the pieces, spray with oil then cook for another 6 minutes.
10. Raise to 400◦F and cook on each side for 2 minutes.
11. Serve on buns with a mayonnaise dollop and 2 pickle chips.
12. Enjoy.

Nutritional Information

Calories: 281, Total Fat: 6g, Saturated Fat: 1g, Total Carbs: 38g, Net Carbs: 37g, Protein: 15g, Sugar: 5g, Fiber: 1g, Sodium: 984mg, Potassium: 288g

Air fryer pork loin

Have you ever tried air fryer pork loin? It is actually quick and very easy to prepare plus you can use your favorite seasonings. The pork loin comes out crispy and perfectly flavored on the outside and very tender on the inside.

Prep time: 5 minutes, **Cook time**: 18minutes; **Serves**:8

Ingredients

1 tbsp garlic powder

1 tbsp salt

1 tbsp basil

3 tbsp brown sugar

2 lb pork loin

Preparation Method

1. Mix all the seasonings in a mixing bowl then press the mixture on all sides of the pork loin.
2. Put the pork in the air fryer basket and set the air fryer to 400°F for 8 minutes.
3. Open the air fryer lid and flip the pork loins. Cook for an additional 10 minutes.
4. Let sit for 5 minutes before slicing and serving. Enjoy.

Nutritional Information

Calories 168, Total Fat 5g, Saturated Fat 1g, Total Carbs 5g, Net Carbs 4g, Protein 25g, Sugar4g, Fiber 1g, Sodium 348mg, Potassium435mg

Air fryer Baked Potatoes

If you have never made air fryer baked potatoes you don't know what you have been missing. Whether you want these potatoes for dinner or any other meal, trust me, you will never make them any other way. The air-fried potatoes are so amazing with crispy skin and tender inside.

Prep time: 10 minutes, **Cook time**: 45minutes; **Serves**: 4

Ingredients

4 large potatoes

3 tbsp olive oil

2 tbsp sea salt

Preparation Method

1. Wash the potatoes then use a fork to poke them all around. Pat them dry with a paper towel.
2. Generously rub each potato with olive oil then sprinkle salt.
3. Place the potatoes in the air fryer basket without overlapping.
4. Close the lid and set to 400ᵒF for 45 minutes. At 35 minutes, poke the potatoes with a fork to check if the center is tender.
5. When the time has elapsed take the potatoes out from the air fryer. Slice them and fluff up the inside. Enjoy.

Nutritional Information

Calories 185, Total Fat 7g, Saturated Fat 1g, Total Carbs 26g, Net Carbs 21g, Protein 5g, Sugar 1g, Fiber 5g, Sodium 3506mg, Potassium 879

Crispy Breaded Pork Chops in the Air fryer

If looking for something different to serve your family or friends coming over then these pork chops are the best. You can make them in the oven but air fryer pork chops are quicker and crispier with the bread adhering better.

Prep time: 10 minutes, **Cook time**: 12 minutes; **Serves**: 6

Ingredients

Olive oil spray

5 6 ¾ inch pork chops, center cut, boneless and fat trimmed

Koser salt

½ cup panko crumbs

⅓ cup crushed cornflakes crumbs

2 tbsp parmesan cheese, grated

1 ¼ tbsp sweet paprika

½ tbsp garlic powder

½ tbsp onion powder

¼ tbsp chili powder

⅛ tbsp black pepper

1 egg, beaten

Preparation Method

1. Preheat the air fryer to 400°F for 12 minutes and spray the basket with oil.
2. Season the pork with salt on both sides. In a mixing bowl, combine crumbs, cheese, paprika, garlic, onion powder, chili, salt, and black pepper.
3. Beat the egg in a separate bowl. Dip the pork chops in the egg then in the crumb mixture.
4. Place 3 chops in the prepared basket and spritz the top with olive oil.
5. Cook for 12 minutes turning halfway through the cooking time. Set aside and repeat with all the pork chops. Serve and enjoy.

Nutritional Information

Calories 378, Total Fat 13g, Saturated Fat 2g, Total Carbs 8g, Net Carbs 7g, Protein33g, Fiber 1g, Sodium 373mg

Crispy Air-fried Tofu

Every tofu eater has this conundrum at some point; how do I make my tofu crispier? This is because they know the magic of crispy tofu and the turmoil of doing it wrong. The air fryer makes your tofu quick and just right.

Prep time: 30 minutes, **Cook time**: 15minutes; **Serves**: 4

Ingredients

16 oz block tofu, extra firm

2 tbsp soy sauce

1 tbsp sesame oil

1 tbsp olive oil

1 clove garlic, minced

Preparation Method

1. Use a tofu press to press tofu for at least 15 minutes. Cut the tofu into bite-size pieces then transfer to a mixing bowl.
2. In a separate bowl add all other ingredients and drizzle the mixture over tofu. Toss to coat then let marinate for 15 minutes.
3. Preheat your air fryer to 375°F and add tofu to the air fryer basket without overlapping.
4. Cook for 15 minutes shaking the basket occasionally for even cooking
5. Serve and enjoy.

Nutritional Information

Calories 212, Total Fat 15.7g, Saturated Fat 2.3g, Total Carbs 5.2g, Net Carbs 2.8g, Protein 16.5g, Sugar 0.2g, Fiber 2.4, Sodium 465mg, Potassium 260mg

Air fryer Rotisserie Chicken

If you hosting a dinner party, try this rotisserie chicken with classic moist texture and lovely burnished skin. Cooking the whole chicken in the air fryer makes the dinner party preparations even easier by freeing your oven space for rolls, casseroles and other dishes. Serve the chicken with your favorite vegetables for a healthy meal.

Prep time: 10 minutes, **Cook time**: 1 hour 10 minutes; **Serves**: 6

Ingredients

4 sprigs thyme, fresh

1 lemon, halved

4 lb whole chicken, giblets removed

¾ tbsp salt, divided

½ tbsp ground pepper, divided

Preparation Method

1. Place thyme and lemon halves in the chicken cavity.
2. Use kitchen twine to truss the chicken legs closed then sprinkle the breasts and legs with half salt and pepper. Place the chicken in the air fryer basket breast side up.
3. Set the air fryer to 350∘F for 30 minutes. Turn the chicken carefully and cook for an additional 15 minutes. Turn the chicken once more and cook for 15 more minutes.
4. Transfer the chicken to a cutting board and let it rest for 10 minutes to cook.
5. Discard the thyme sprigs and reserve the lemon wedges.
6. Sprinkle the remaining salt and pepper then squeeze the juice from preserved lemons over the chicken. Serve and enjoy.

Nutritional Information

Calories 166, Total Fat 6.4g, Saturated Fat 1.8g, Total Carbs 1, Net Carbs 0.6, Protein 24.8g, Sugar, Fiber 0.4g, Sodium 364mg, Potassium 225mg

Air Fryer Scallops

Air fryer scallops make an impressive quick dinner that will win you and your family over. Be careful to cook the scallops to temperature. The scallops may not turn golden brown to tell you they are ready so do not wait for a golden-brown crust. Serve the scallops with lemon herb sauce for a zest in each bite.

Prep time: 5 minutes, **Cook time**: 20 minutes; **Serves**:2

Ingredients

8 scallops, cleaned and patted dry

⅛ tbsp salt

¼ tbsp ground pepper

Cooking spray

¼ cup extra virgin olive oil

2 tbsp flat-leaf parsley, finely chopped

2 tbsp capers, finely chopped

1 tbsp lemon zest, finely grated

½ tbsp garlic, finely chopped

Preparation Method

1. Sprinkle the scallops with salt and pepper then coat the air fryer basket with cooking spray.
2. Add the scallops in the basket and coat them with cooking spray.
3. Cook the scallops at 400°F for 6 minutes.
4. Combine olive oil, parsley, capers, lemon zest, and chopped garlic in a mixing bowl. Drizzle the mixture over the scallops, serve and enjoy.

Nutritional Information

Calories 348, Total Fat 29.8g, Saturated Fat 4.2g, Total Carbs 4.6g, Net Carbs 4.2g, Protein 13.9g, Fiber 0.4g, Sodium 660mg, Potassium 260mg

Air Fryer Salmon with Horseradish Rub

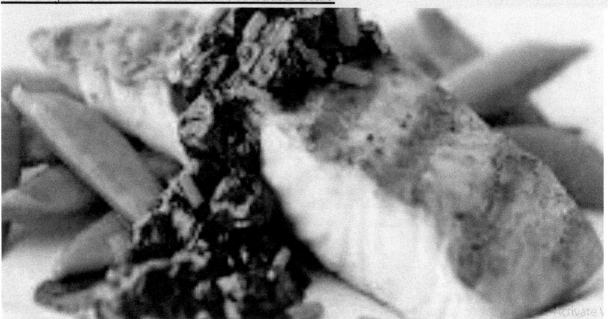

A crispy crust of horseradish, flat-leaf parsley, and capers on salmon is all you need to serve yourself and your family for a comforting dinner. If fresh horseradish isn't available, use a high-quality product ensuring you drain and squeeze it for minimal moisture.

Prep time: 10 minutes, **Cook time**: 20 minutes; **Serves**: 2

Ingredients

Cooking spray

2 tbsp horseradish, finely grated

1 tbsp flat-leaf parsley

1 tbsp capers, finely chopped

1 tbsp extra virgin oil

12 oz salmon fillet

¼ tbsp salt

¼ tbsp ground pepper

Preparation Method

1. Coat the air fryer with cooking spray.
2. In a mixing bowl, combine horseradish, parsley, chopped capers, and oil.
3. Sprinkle salt and pepper over salmon fillet then spread horseradish mixture over the salmon.
4. Coat with cooking spray then place the salmon in the air fryer basket.
5. Cook at 375∘F for 15 minutes. When the time has elapsed, let the salmon rest for 5 minutes before serving.

Nutritional Information

Calories 305, Total Fat 14.7g, Saturated Fat 2.7g, Total Carbs 7.2g, Net Carbs 4.6g, Protein 35.2g, Sugar 2g, Fiber 2.9g, Sodium 482mg, Potassium 787mg

Air fryer Salmon Cake

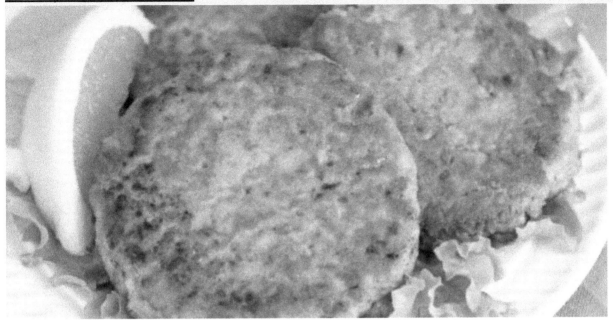

These salmon patties are my reminiscent of crispy on the outside, classic salmon croquettes which are delicious and pillowy tender on the inside. Air fryer salmon cakes are easy to make and loved by kids, grown-ups love them too. Look for many varieties of salmon and don't be afraid ones with bones. The bones are easy to remove.

Prep time: 10 minutes, **Cook time**: 15 minutes; **Serves**: 2

Ingredients

Cooking spray

15 oz can pink salmon, unsalted

½ cup panko breadcrumbs, whole wheat

2 tbsp dill, freshly chopped

2 tbsp canola mayonnaise

2 tbsp Dijon mustard

¼ tbsp ground pepper

1 egg

2 lemon wedges

Preparation Method

1. Coat the air fryer basket with cooking spray.
2. Drain the salmon, remove and discard the skin and bones. Place the salmon in a mixing bowl then add breadcrumbs, dill, mayonnaise, mustard, and pepper. Stir until well combined.
3. Shape the mixture into 4 cakes.
4. Coat the cakes with cooking spray and arrange them in the prepared basket.
5. Cook at 400∘F for 12 minutes. Serve and enjoy.

Nutritional Information

Calories 517, Total Fat 26.7g, Saturated Fat 5g, Total Carbs 14.7g, Net Carbs 12.6g, Protein 51.8g, Fiber 2.1g, Sodium 384mg, Potassium 680mg

Air Fryer Everything Bagel Chicken roll-ups

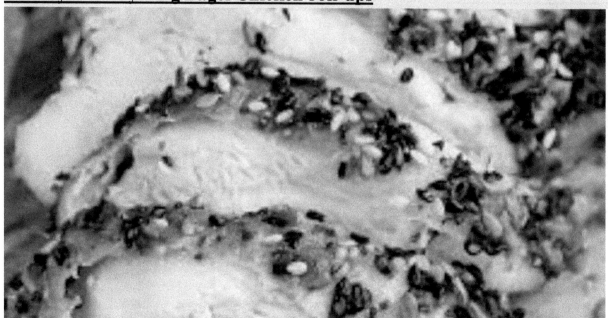

Imagine cozy, very easy to make tantalizing chicken rolls ups coated in crunch everything bagel seasoning on your dinner table after a long and tiring working day. I would definitely love it and I think everyone would want that. This chicken is an absolute winner in my household so try and I bet you will love it.

Prep time: 15 minutes, **Cook time**: 15 minutes; **Serves**: 8

Ingredients

¼ cup everything bagel seasoning

½ cup sesame seeds

2 egg whites

½ cup whipped cream cheese

½ cup cheddar cheese, reduced-fat and shredded

¼ cup scallions, chopped

8 chicken breasts cutlets

½ cup baby spinach. Chopped

Olive oil spray

Preparation Method

1. Combine everything bagel seasoning and sesame seeds in a mixing bowl.
2. Place the egg whites in a separate bowl. Preheat your air fryer to 375ºF.
3. In a separate bowl, mix cream cheese, cheese, and scallions until well combined.
4. Place the chicken on a cutting board then spread the 1.5tbsp of the cheese mixture on each chicken cutlet. Place 1 tbsp of spinach at the center of each chicken cutlet then roll up each chicken cutlet and place the seam side down.
5. Dredge the roll-ups in egg whites then in the sesame seeds mixture, each at a time.
6. Place the batches in the air fryer basket and spray cooking spray.

7. Cook for 15 minutes or until crispy and golden, making sure you turn halfway through the cooking time.
8. When the time has elapsed, transfer the roll-ups in serving platters and enjoy.

Nutritional Information

Calories 397, Total Fat 16g, Saturated Fat 5g, Total Carbs 8g, Net Carbs 4g, Protein 53g, Sugar 0g, Fiber 4g, Sodium 368mg, Potassium 1028mg

Air fryer Garlic Rosemary Brussels Sprouts

It's surprisingly amazing what the air fryer can do to Brussel sprouts. Unlike in a pan or skillet, these brussels sprouts are low in fat and awesomely crispy. They are easy, very quick and healthy go-to dinner dish that's perfect for your thanksgiving evening party.

Prep time: 15 minutes, **Cook time**: 20 minutes; **Serves**:4

Ingredients

3 tbsp olive oil

2 garlic cloves

½ tbsp salt

¼ tbsp pepper

1 lb Brussel sprouts, trimmed and halved

½ cup panko breadcrumbs

1 ½ tbsp rosemary, freshly minced

Preparation Method

1. Preheat your air fryer to 350°F.
2. Place the first four ingredients in a microwave-safe bowl and microwave for 30 seconds.
3. Toss the Brussel sprouts in 2 tbsp of the oil mixture until well coated.
4. Transfer the Brussel sprouts to an air fryer and cook for 5 minutes. Stir the Brussel sprouts and cook for 8 more minutes or until lightly browned.
5. Toss the breadcrumbs with fresh rosemary and remaining oil mixture. Sprinkle the mixture over the Brussel sprouts and continue cooking until the sprouts are tender and browned about five minutes.
6. Serve with your favorite side and enjoy.

Nutritional Information

Calories 164, Total Fat 11g, Saturated Fat 1g, Total Carbs 15g, Net Carbs11g, Protein 0g, Sugar 3g, Fiber 4g, Sodium 342mg

Cauliflower Taco Bowl

This is a healthy and quick recipe especially when meat is prepared ahead of time. To give this dinner recipe a great taste, use smoked paprika. Its is an easy meal to prepare.   **Prep time**: 10 minutes, **Cook time**: 15 minutes; **Serves** 2

Ingredients

2 cups cauliflower florets, frozen

1½ cups turkey, ground

Smoked paprika to taste

Optional toppings

1 chopped tomato

1 cup chopped lettuce

Fresh cilantro to taste

⅓ cup shredded cheese

Preparation Method

1. Use the package directions to thaw the cauliflower in a microwave or air fry them for about 15 minutes in an air fryer at 400°F.
2. If thawing, place half the bag in a refrigerator for another time.
3. Pour the other half in a medium bowl and splash with paprika.
4. Reheat frozen and prepared taco meat then add to the bowl.
5. Top with favorite toppings.
6. Serve and enjoy.

Nutritional Information

Calories: 306, Total Fat: 10g, Saturated fat: 5g, Total carbs: 9g, Net carbs: 6g, Protein: 57g, Sugar: 4g, Fiber: 3g, Sodium: 240mg, Potassium: 1012mg

Crispy Veggie Quesadillas in an Air Fryer

Looking for a satisfying and quick weeknight supper? This is your recipe as these Quesadillas pair well with beer, ice-cold, it is also a healthy recipe as black beans bring fiber and protein to your party.

Prep time: 20 minutes, **Cook time**: 20 minutes; **Serves** 4

Ingredients

4, 6-inch, flour tortillas, sprouted whole-grain

4 oz shredded sharp cheddar cheese, reduced-fat

1 cup red bell pepper, sliced

1 cup zucchini, sliced

1 cup drained canned black beans, rinsed and no-salt added

Cooking spray

2 oz plain Greek yogurt, reduced-fat

1 tbsp lime zest + 1 tbsp fresh lime juice

¼ tbsp ground cumin

2 tbsp fresh cilantro, chopped

½ cup pico de gallo, drained and refrigerated

Preparation Method

1. Splash 2 tbsp cheese over each tortilla half placed on a flat work surface.
2. Top ¼ cup red pepper slices, black beans, and zucchini slices on each tortilla.
3. Splash with ½ cup remaining cheese then fold over the tortillas to form quesadillas, half-moon shaped.
4. Coat the quesadillas lightly using cooking spray. Secure using toothpicks.
5. Prepared your air fryer basket by spraying with cooking spray then place 2 quesadillas into it.

6. Cook for about 10 minutes at 400◦F until slightly crispy, golden brown, cheese, melts, and slightly softened vegetables. Turn over the quesadillas halfway through.
7. Repeat for the remaining quesadillas.
8. Meanwhile, place the lime juice, lime zest, cumin, and yogurt in a bowl, small, then stir together.
9. Cut the quesadillas to wedges and splash each with cilantro.
10. Serve each quesadilla with 1tbsp cumin cream and 2 tbsp pico de gallo.
11. Enjoy.

Nutritional Information

Calories: 291, Total fat: 8g, Saturated fat: 4g, Total carbs: 36g, Net carbs: 28g, Protein: 17g, Sugar: 3g, Fiber: 8g, Sodium: 518mg, Potassium: 654mg

Ninja Foodi Air Fryer Crispy Chicken Wings

Preparing chicken wings in your air fryer is much easy and affordable than buying them in a restaurant. You can also use different elements for different flavors.make sure you try these chicken wings for you and your family.

Prep time: 5minutes, **Cook time**:30 minutes; **Serves**:12 chicken wings

Ingredients

12 chicken wingettes

½ cup chicken broth

¼ cup melted butter

Season all

Preparation Method

1. Add the chicken wings in a pot and add the chicken broth.
2. Close the lid and set the valve to sealing. set timer for 8 minutes.
3. When the time has elapsed, quick-release pressure and transfer the chicken wings to an air fryer basket.
4. Pour melted butter on the wings and mix the wings gently to coat them.
5. Sprinkle season all then close the air fryer lid. Air crisp for 10 minutes, mix the wings and air fry for 10 more minutes.
6. Serve and enjoy.

Nutritional Information

Calories 431, Total Fat 28g, Saturated Fat 9g, Total Carbs 0g, Net Carbs 0g, Protein 43g, Sugar 0g, Fiber 0g, Sodium 179mg, Potassium

Air fryer Buffalo Chicken Pull-Apart Bread

Are looking for a snack or appetizer to break up the day? If so, grab that loaf of bread, slice it, stuff it and bake it to cheesy perfection. There you go you! Your snack is done. For me, the cheese paired with bread threw it over the top. I would simply say this is my go-to easy snack that will please you or your crowd.

Prep time: 15 minutes, **Cook time**: 5 minutes; **Serves**: 10

Ingredients

Round sourdough bread, slice diagonally into 1-inch cubes

1 cup mozzarella	2 tbsp butter, melted
1 lb buffalo chicken, shredded	½ cup crumbled blue cheese
8 slices Monterey Jack Cheese	1 green onion, chopped

Preparation Method

1. Preheat your air fryer to 400ᵒF for 5 minutes.
2. Place mozzarella cheese on each bread cube then place buffalo chicken on mozzarella cheese.
3. Place Monterey jack cheese on the chicken and coat the bread with butter.
4. Place on the metal rack in the lowest position.
5. Cook for the 5 minutes or until the cheese has melted.
6. Top with blue cheese and green onions. Enjoy

Nutritional Information

Calories 130, Total Fat 8g, Saturated Fat 5g, Total Carbs 2g, Net Carbs 2g, Protein 11g, Sugar 0g, Fiber 0g, Sodium 278mg

Air fryer Blooming Onion

The crispy batter paired with the tender onion is love at first bite. You never have to leave your home for the restaurant to have booming onions when you have an air fryer in your household. Serve the onions with dipping sauce for an outstanding snack or appetizer.

Prep time: 2 hours, **Cook time**: 20 minutes; **Serves**:6

Ingredients

1 onion, peeled and top cut off

2 eggs

2 tbsp milk

1 cup panko bread crumbs

1 tbsp paprika

1 tbsp garlic powder

Olive oil

Preparation Method

1. Place the cut side down of the onion and cut it into 8 slices.
2. Place the onion in ice-cold water for 2 hours, face side down.
3. In a mixing bowl, beat together egg and milk.
4. Mix bread crumbs and seasoning in another mixing bowl.
5. Coat the onion with the egg mixture then sprinkle panko bread crumbs all over the onion.
6. Place in the air fryer basket and spray with olive oil.
7. Cook in the air fryer at 390◦F for 10 minutes.
8. If not crispy enough cook for 5 more minutes. Serve and enjoy.

Nutritional Information

Calories 130, Total Fat 5g, Saturated Fat 1g, Total Carbs 16g, Net Carbs 15g, Protein 5g, Sugar 2g, Fiber 1g, Sodium 159mg

Ninja Foodi and Air Fryer Bacon Wrapped Hot Dogs

These air fryer wrapped hot dogs are a real step up from the common hotdogs. They are flavorful, juicy, crispy and above all easy to make. Trust me these hot dogs will blow you and your friends away. Serve these bacon-wrapped hot dogs with a burn or skip the bun for a low carb snack

Prep time: 10 minutes, **Cook time**: 12 minutes; **Serves**:6

Ingredients

6 hot dogs

6 slices of bacon

Preparation Method

1. Wrap each hot dog with a bacon slice; roll from one end to another.
2. Place the hot dogs in an air fryer basket then cook at 390ᵒF for 12 minutes. Turn the hot dogs in the middle of the cooking period.
3. Serve and enjoy.

Nutritional Information

Calories 208, Total Fat 18g, Saturated Fat 7g, Total Carbs 1g, Net Carbs 1g, Protein 10g, Sugar 1g, Fiber 0g, Sodium 603mg

Ninja Foodi Chocolate Oatmeal

This chocolate oatmeal is basically simple and can be served as a dessert or as a breakfast but it's just amazing either way. It is an ultimate yum when topped with strawberries and chocolate chips. Everyone will absolutely love it.

Prep time: 5 minutes, **Cook time**: 5 minutes; **Serves** 4

Ingredients

2 cups quick oats

4 cups chocolate almond milk

½ cup chocolate chips

Optional: strawberries

Preparation Method

1. Spray the safe dish inside of the oven with non-stick spray.
2. Add almond milk and quick oats then stir.
3. Add 1½ cups water into the pot with trivet in then place oven safe dish on the trivet.
4. Put the attached pressure cooker lid on and close the steam valve.
5. Set for 5 minutes on high pressure. Quick release pressure and stir.
6. Serve strawberries and chocolate chips.

Nutritional Information

Calories: 296, Total fat: 11g, Saturated fat: 3g, Total carbs: 43g, Net carbs: 38g, Protein: 7g, Sugar: 14g, Fiber: 5g, Sodium: 341mg, Potassium: 143mg

Air fryer Apple Chips

If you are willing to satisfy the sweet cravings, try this. The Apple chips are super easy preparing, crispy, delicious, and a healthy snack made in the air fryer. 8 minutes is all you need and you are done.

Prep time: 5 minutes, **Cook time**: 8 minutes; **Serves** 3

Ingredients

3 crisp apples, large and sweet

¾ tbsp cinnamon, ground

A pinch of salt

Preparation Method

1. Wash the apple thoroughly in apple cider vinegar or warm water.
2. **Optional:** core the apple or leave seeds in.
3. Preheat your air fryer to 390﹏F.
4. Meanwhile, cut apples using a sharp knife into ⅛ -inch rounds sideways.
5. Mix salt and cinnamon in a small bowl.
6. Rub the apple pieces with cinnamon mixture then arrange them in a single layer in your air fryer.
7. Close and cook at 390﹏F for about 8 minutes. Flip half-way through.
8. Repeat for the remaining batches.
9. Once the crispiness is to your liking, place them in a cooling rack to cool.
10. Serve and enjoy or store in a container, air-tight.

Nutritional Information

Calories: 65, Total fat: 0g, Saturated fat: 0g, Total carbs: 18g, Net carbs: 13g, Protein: 24g, Sugar: 11g, Fiber: 5g, Sodium: 4mg, Potassium: 141mg

S'mores In An Air Fryer

This will become one of the summertime favorite treats or anytime all year round. This is an ultimate dessert that you will make over and over for family treat whether a party treat or a midnight snack. You will fall in love with it.

Prep time: 2 minutes, **Cook time**: 8 minutes; **Serves** 2

Ingredients

Graham crackers , half broken

Marshmallows

Hersey bars, same size to Graham Cracker pieces

Preparation Method

1. Place the crackers halves into the basket of your air fryer.
2. Top marshmallow on each cracker half.
3. Cook for about 7-8 minutes at 390◦F until marshmallows begin to crisp up.
4. Carefully remove marshmallows then place Hersey bars on top.
5. Place the crackers on top gently pushing down.
6. Serve immediately and enjoy.

Nutritional Information

Calories: 176, Total fat: 8g, Saturated fat: 4g, Total carbs: 26g, Net carbs: 25g, Protein: 2g, Sugar: 18g, Fiber: 1g, Sodium: 72mg, Potassium: 111mg

Mexican Air Fryer Corn on the Cob

This is a juicy dish made in just 10 minutes and perfect for gluten-free, vegan, and low carb diets. Mexican air fryer corn on the cob makes a great snack or a perfect side dish to tacos, burgers, fish and grilled chicken.

Prep time: 2 minutes, **Cook time**: 10 minutes; **Serves** 3

Ingredients

3 corn on cob

Spray, low-calorie

Toppings

Salt

Lemon zest

Cilantro, chopped

Fresh coriander

Preparation Method

1. Preheat your air fryer to 200◦C or 400◦F.
2. Spray the corn with low -calorie spray placed in a bowl then season with salt.
3. Place the seasoned corn on the cob into an air fryer basket.
4. Cook for about 10 minutes. Turn severally for even cooking.
5. Remove and top with lemon zest, extra salt and cilantro or coriander.
6. Serve and enjoy.

Nutritional Information

Calories: 77, Total fat: 1g, Saturated fat: 0g, Total carbs: 16g, Net carbs: 15g, Protein: 2g, Sugar: 5g, Fiber: 1g, Sodium: 13mg, Potassium: 243mg

Air Fryer Sweet Potato Tots

Preparing this recipe in an air fryer yields a soft interior and a crisp exterior thus a great dish that will be enjoyed by everyone, including your kids. The sweet potato tots are a perfect way to bring veggies into your meal.

Prep time: 20 minutes, **Cook time**: 1 hour, **Serves** 4

Ingredients

14 oz peeled sweet potatoes

1 tbsp potato starch

⅛ tbsp garlic powder

1¼ tbsp divided kosher salt

¾ cup ketchup, no-salt added

Cooking spray

Preparation Method

1. Boil water in a medium pot over high heat.
2. Add potatoes and cook for about 15 minutes until fork tender.
3. Transfer into a plate and cool for 15 minutes.
4. Grate the potatoes over a bowl, medium, then toss with garlic powder, potato starch, and 1 tbsp salt.
5. Shape the mixture into 24 cylinders, 1-inch tot-shaped.
6. Coat your air fryer lightly with cooking spray then add 12 tots in one layer and spray using cooking spray .
7. Cook for about 12-14 minutes at 400₀F until browned lightly. Remove and splash with ⅛ tbsp salt. Repeat for the remaining tots. Serve with ketchup. Enjoy!

Nutritional Information

Calories: 78, Total fat: 0g, Saturated fat: 0g, Total carbs: 19g, Net carbs: 17g, Protein: 1g, Sugar: 8g, Fiber: 2g, Sodium: 335mg, Potassium: 239mg

Air Fryer Doughnuts

If you have doughnuts cravings with no guilt, then these deliver the same tender, crackly sugar glazed and sweet goodness. Thanks to air fryer for this amazing recipe that might become one of your favorite snack recipes.everyone will enjoy.

Prep time: 35 minutes, **Cook time**: 1 hour 45 minutes; **Serves** 8

Ingredients

¼ cup warm water, 100°F

1 tbsp dry yeast, active

¼ cup + ½ tbsp divided granulated sugar

2 cups all-purpose flour, 8½ oz

¼ tbsp kosher salt

¼ cup whole milk, room temperature

2 tbsp melted butter, unsalted

1 beaten egg, large

1 cup, 4 oz, powdered sugar

4 tbsp tap water

Preparation Method

1. Place water, ½ tbsp sugar, and yeast in a bowl, small, then stir together. Let sit for about 5 minutes until stir.
2. Combine flour ¼ cup sugar, and salt in a bowl, medium, then add yeast mixture, butter, egg, and milk.
3. Stir using a spoon, wooden, until dough comes together and is soft. Transfer onto a surface that is lightly floured.

4. Knead for about 1-2 minutes until smooth then transfer into a greased bowl, lightly, and cover. Let rise for about 1 hour until volume doubled.
5. Now place the raised dough on a surface lightly floured then cut 8 doughnuts form it. Use a round cutter, 3-inch, and 1-inch to remove the center.
6. Transfer the cut doughnuts and holes on a surface lightly floured then wrap loosely with plastic wrap and let sit for about 30 minutes until doubled.
7. Layer 2 doughnuts and 2 holes in an air fryer basket then cook for about 4-5 minutes at 400◦F until golden brown.
8. Repeat for the remaining doughnuts and doughnut holes.
9. Meanwhile, whisk together water and sugar in a bowl, medium, until smooth.
10. Dip doughnuts and holes to coat then place on a rack, wire, to drip off excess glaze.
11. Let sit for 10 minutes for glaze to harden.
12. Serve and enjoy.

Nutritional Information

Calories: 238, Total fat: 4g, Saturated fat: 2g, Total carbs: 46g, Net carbs: 45g, Protein: 5g, Sugar: 22g, Fiber: 1g, Sodium: 74mg, Potassium: 123mg

Air Fryer Banana Bread

Brimming with tradition banana flavor? Have a banana bread slice with a butter smear for an afternoon snack and you will be amazed. The dense texture of banana bread is just wonderful and have a deepen flavor when walnuts are toasted before used in the recipe.

Prep time: 15 minutes, **Cook time:** 45 minutes; **Serves 8**

Ingredients

3 oz wheat flour, white-whole

1 tbsp cinnamon

½ tbsp kosher salt

¼ tbsp baking soda

12 oz mashed ripe bananas

2 lightly-beaten eggs, large

½ cup granulated sugar

Preparation Method

1. Line a parchment paper on the bottom of a round cake pan, 6-inch, then coat with cooking spray. Whisk cinnamon, flour, baking soda, and salt together in a bowl, medium, and set aside.
2. Whisk together eggs, bananas, yoghurt, sugar, vanilla, and oil in another medium bowl.
3. Pour wet mixture into the flour mixture then stir until combined well.
4. Now pour the batter into the pan and splash with walnuts.
5. Heat your air fryer, 5.3-quart, at 310°F then insert the pan in.
6. Cook for about 30 -35 minutes until browned. Make sure a toothpick comes out clean when inserted into the middle.turn halfway through.
7. Transfer and cool the bread on a wire rack for about 15 minutes. Slices and serve. Enjoy!

Nutritional Information

Calories: 180, Total fat: 6g, Saturated fat: 1g, Total carbs: 29g, Net carbs: 27g, Protein: 4g, Sugar: 17g, Fiber: 2g, Sodium: 184mg, Potassium: 98mg

Air-fried Butter Cake

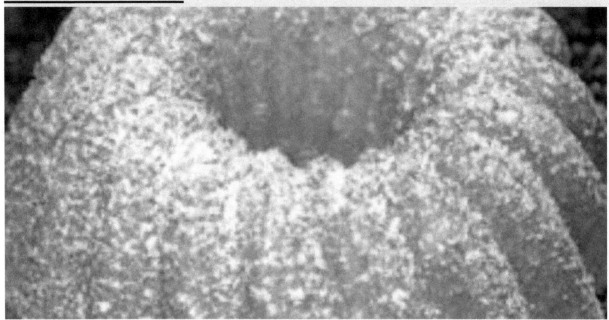

This is a really easy recipe to make with a very nice consistency though it's just a basic butter cake. When prepared in an air fryer, it comes out perfectly and will leave you craving for more. It makes a perfect dessert .

Prep time: 10 minutes, **Cook time**: 15 minutes; **Serves** 4

Ingredients

Cooking spray	1 egg
7 tbsp butter, room temperature	1⅔ cups flour, all-purpose
¼ cup white sugar	Salt to taste
2 tbsp white sugar	6 tbsp milk

Preparation Method

1. Preheat your air fryer to 350◦F then spray tube pan, small-fluted, using cooking spray.
2. Whisk together ¼ cup sugar and 2 tbsp butter in a medium bowl until creamy and light. Use a mixer, electric one, to whisk.
3. Add egg then mix until fluffy and smooth.
4. Stir in salt and flour then milk. Mix the batter thoroughly.
5. Transfer the batter into prepared pan then level the surface with a spoon back.
6. Place pan in the basket of your air fryer and cover.
7. Cook for about 15 minutes until a toothpick comes out clean when inserted at the center.
8. Remove the cake from the air fryer and cool for 5 minutes. Serve and enjoy.

Nutritional Information

Calories: 470, Total fat: 22.4g, Saturated fat: 14g, Total carbs: 59.7g, Net carbs: 58.3g, Protein: 7.9g, Sugar: 20g, Fiber: 1.4g, Sodium: 210mg, Potassium: 113mg

RED MEAT RECIPES

Air Fryer Steak

No need to grill steak anymore when you can get a tender, crispy steak in just 18 minutes. Let me attest that I am not a steak lover but this roast beef won me over and changed me. The secret is preheating your air fryer and flipping the steak halfway the cooking time for crispness on both sides.

Prep time: 15 minutes, **Cook time**: 18 minutes; **Serves**:4

Ingredients

1 tbsp salt, coarsely ground

¼ tbsp chili powder

¼ tbsp pepper

1 tbsp garlic powder

½ tbsp onion powder

2 steaks

6 strips bacon

Preparation Method

1. Combine the seasonings in a mixing bowl then lay the steak on a chopping board and sprinkle seasoning on both sides.
2. Lay three pieces of the bacon horizontally, lined up next to each other without overlapping.
3. Wrap the top piece of bacon around and under the steak then repeat the same with the second piece of bacon. Pull the last side up of the third bacon piece and tuck it under the second piece so they don't unravel.
4. Repeat the process with the second steak then lay the wrapped steak in the air fryer.
5. Preheat your air fryer at 375◦F for 5 minutes then set a total time of 18 minutes.
6. Flip the steak when halfway the cooking time for even cooking.
7. Let the steak rest for 5 minutes before serving. Enjoy.

Nutritional Information

Calories 377, Total Fat 29g, Saturated Fat 11g, Total Carbs 1g, Net Carbs 1g, Protein 27g, Fiber 0g, Sodium 2024mg, Potassium 377mg

Air Fryer Roast Beef

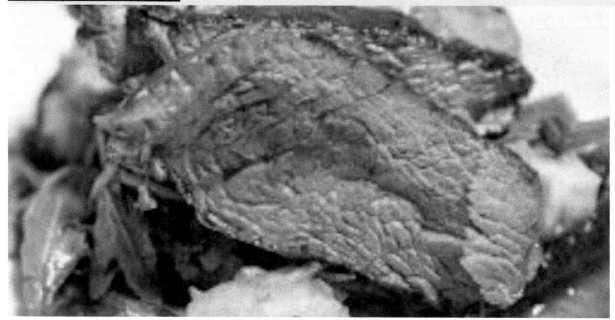

Anyone who owns an air fryer knows that it can do much more than frying. It cooks faster than a conventional oven. This toast beef is a real boon; it takes 35 minutes in the air fryer so perfect when you extremely hungry and pressed for time

Prep time: 5 minutes, **Cook time**: 35 minutes; **Serves**:7

Ingredients

2 lb beef roast

Oil

Rub

1 tbsp kosher salt

1 tbsp black pepper

2 tbsp garlic powder

1 tbsp summer savory

Preparation Method

1. Mix the rub ingredients and rub the mixture on the beef roast.
2. Place the roast in the air fryer fat side down the spray with oil.
3. Set your air fryer at 400ᵒF for 35 minutes. When the steak has cooked for 20 minutes, flip it and brush with some oil then cook for the remaining 15 minutes.
4. Remove the beef roast from the air fryer and let it rest for 10 minutes to cool.
5. Serve and enjoy.

Nutritional Information

Calories 238, Total Fat 14g, Saturated Fat 6g, Total Carbs 1g, Net Carbs 1g, Protein 25g, Fiber 0g, Sodium 1102mg, Potassium 448mg

Air Fryer Mongolian Beef

Looking for a favorite air fryer dinner recipe? Air fryer Mongolian beef is one of the recipes that you can't afford to miss at your dinner table. It is a healthy recipe as it is gluten-free and super easy as it requires only 10 minutes to be ready.

Prep time: 20 minutes, Cook time: 20 minutes; Serves 4

Ingredients

For meat

1 lb flank steak, thinly sliced ¼ cup corn starch

For sauce

2 tbsp vegetable oil ½ cup soy sauce

½ tbsp ginger ½ cup water

1 tbsp minced garlic ¾ cup packed brown sugar

For Extras

Cooked rice Green onions

Green beans

Preparation Method

1. Coat steak with corn starch then place in an Air Fryer. Cook for about 5 minutes per side at 390°F. Meanwhile, place all sauce ingredients in a saucepan, medium, over high-medium heat. Warm while whisking until a low boil.
2. Place sauce mixture and steak in a bowl then let steak soak in the sauce for 5-10 minutes.
3. Remove steak using tongs letting excess sauce drizzle. Place over green beans and rice.
4. Top with sauce and serve. Enjoy!

Nutritional Information

Calories: 441, Total Fat: 16.3g, Saturated fat: 5.3g, Total carbs: 39.3g, Net carbs: 38.9g, Protein: 33.8g, Sugar: 27g, Fiber: 0.4g, Sodium: 1870mg, Potassium: 506mg

Air Fryer Korean BBQ Beef

Air fryer Korean BBQ beef is one of the recipes that you would think of ordering out though you prepare it at your home. Pompeian white wine vinegar is a perfect addition to this recipe as it has a crisp clean taste and has og sugar.

Prep time: 15 minutes, **Cook time**: 30 minutes; **Serves** 6

Ingredients

1 lb thinly sliced flank steak

¼ cup corn starch

Coconut spray, Pompeian oils

For Sauce

½ cup soy sauce

½ cup brown sugar

2 tbsp Pompeian White wine vinegar

1 minced garlic clove

1 tbsp hot chili sauce

1 tbsp ginger, Ground

½ tbsp sesame seeds

1 tbsp cornstarch

1 tbsp water

Preparation Method

1. Toss steak slices with cornstarch.In the meantime, spray the air fryer basket with oil spray.
2. Place steak slices in the basket and coat on top with oil spray.
3. Cook at 390ₒF for about 10 minutes. Flip the slices and cook for another 10 minutes.
4. Meanwhile, place all the sauce ingredients except cornstarch in a saucepan, medium, then warm until a low boil. Add water and cornstarch then whisk.
5. Remove the steak carefully and pour over the sauce.Top with green beans, green onions, and cooked rice. Serve and enjoy.

Nutritional Information

Calories: 487, Total fat: 22g, Saturated fat: 10g, Total carbs: 32g, Net carbs: 30g, Protein: 39g, Sugar: 21g, Fiber: 2g, Sodium: 1531mg, Potassium: 891mg

Air Fryer Cheesy Beef Enchiladas

Cheesy beef enchiladas are a perfect way to enjoy dinner every night. This recipe comes out perfectly when prepared in an air fryer a well as having a great flavor. Everyone including your kids will love it.

Prep time: 20 minutes, **Cook time**: 10 minutes; **Serves 8**

Ingredients

1 lb ground beef

1 package taco seasoning

8 tortillas, Gluten-free

1 can drained and rinsed black beans

1 can drained and diced tomatoes

1 can drained mild chopped Green chilies

1 can red Enchilada Sauce

1 cup Mexican cheese, shredded

1 cup fresh cilantro, chopped

½ cup sour cream

Preparation Method

1. Brown the beef in a skillet, medium-sized, then add taco Seasoning as per package seasonings.
2. Build tortillas by adding each with beef, tomatoes, beans, and chilies then place each tortilla in your air fryer basket.
3. Pour enchilada sauce evenly over tortillas in the air fryer then top evenly with cheese.
4. Cook for about 5 minutes at 355₀F.
5. Remove carefully and top with your favorite toppings.
6. Serve and enjoy!

Nutritional Information

Calories: 454, Total Fat: 20g, Saturated fat: 8g, Total carbs: 40g, Net carbs: 34g, Protein: 27g, Sugar: 2g, Fiber: 6g, Sodium: 655mg, Potassium: 419mg

Air Fryer Glazed Steaks, Gluten-Free

This are delicious Air Fryer Glazed Steaks that are easy to prepare with great flavor. This recipe makes a great and a hearty dinner giving you all the reasons to enjoy. It is a

Prep time: 4 hours 20 minutes, **Cook time:** 20 minutes; **Serves** 2

Ingredients

2,6oz, sirloin steaks

2 tbsp soy sauce

½ tbsp Worcestershire sauce

2 tbsp brown sugar

1 tbsp peeled ginger, Grated

1 tbsp crushed garlic

1 tbsp salt, seasoned

Pepper and salt to taste.

Preparation Method

1. Place steak and all other ingredients in a seal-able bag, large, then seal it.
2. Place the bag in the fridge for not less than 8 hours to marinate.
3. Line aluminum foil to the air fryer bottom then spray with cooking spray, non-stick.
4. Add steaks on the prepared foil.
5. Cook for about 10 minutes at 400◦F. Rotate the steaks and cook for another 10-15 minutes until desired doneness.
6. Serve warm and enjoy.

Nutritional Information

Calories: 271, Total fat: 12g, Saturated fat: 5g, Total carbs: 15g, Net carbs: 15, Protein: 25g, Sugar: 11g, Fiber: 0g, Sodium: 1732mg, Potassium: 1231mg

Air Fryer Beef Kabobs

These are soft and juicy skewers that are very easy to prepare and full of flavor. You don't have to use oil that being the best part of using an air fryer. This dish is delicious and kid-friendly meaning everyone will enjoy it.

Prep time: 30 minutes, **Cook time**: 10 minutes; **Serves** 4

Ingredients

1 lb chuck ribs, 1-inch pieces

⅓ cup sour cream, low-fat

2 tbsp soy sauce

8, 6-ich, skewers

1 bell peppers, 1-inch pieces

½ onion, 1-inch pieces

Preparation Method

1. Mix together soy sauce and sour cream in a bowl, medium, then marinate the chuck rib pieces in the sauce mixture for not less than 30 minutes or overnight.
2. meanwhile, soak skewers for 10 minutes in water the thread bell peppers, onions, and beef onto them.
3. Add some black pepper, freshly ground.
4. Cook on a preheated air fryer to 400°F for about 10 minutes. Turn halfway through.
5. Serve and enjoy.

Nutritional Information

Calories: 250, Total Fat: 15g, Saturated fat: 6g, Total carbs: 4g, Net carbs: 2g, Protein: 23g, Sugar: 2g, Fiber: 2g, Sodium: 609mg, Potassium: 519mg

Spicy Lamb Sirloin Steak

If you are looking for a quick recipe, try this and in no time, this air fried recipe is ready. This flavorful lamb sirloin steak is easy and will unleash air fryer full potential and gives you a healthful dish each night.

Prep time: 40 minutes, **Cook time**: 15 minutes; **Serves** 4

Ingredients

½ onion

4 ginger slices

5 garlic cloves

1 tbsp Garam Masala

1 tbsp fennel, ground

1 tbsp cinnamon, ground

½ tbsp cardamom, ground

½ -1 tbsp salt

1 lb lamb sirloin steaks, boneless

Preparation Method

1. Place all ingredients except lamb chops in a blender and blend for 3-4 minutes until all ingredients incorporate well and onion is finely minced.
2. Slash lamb chops with a knife for marinade to easily penetrate then place in a bowl, large.
3. Add blended mixture over lamb chops and place in the refrigerator to rest for about 30 minutes or overnight. Preheat your air fryer to 330°F.
4. Layer lamb chops in the fryer and cook for about 15 minutes. Flip halfway. Make sure lamb chops internal temperature registers 150F when a meat thermometer is inserted. Serve.

Nutritional Information

Calories: 182, Total Fat: 7g, Saturated fat: 2g, Total carbs: 3g, Net carbs: 2g, Protein: 24g, Sugar: 2g, Fiber: 1g, Sodium: 774mg, Potassium: 502mg

Air Fryer Rib Eye Steak With Blue Cheese Butter

There is nothing better than a nice cooked steak giving you a nice treat. The Air fryer rib-eye steak with blue cheese butter is a fabulous meal across your lips. Do not trim steak for optimal results and flavors.

Prep time: 15 minutes, **Cook time**: 7 minutes; **Serves** 2

Ingredients

32 oz Rib Eye Steaks, 2

2 tbsp kosher salt

1½ tbsp black pepper, freshly ground

1 tbsp garlic powder

2 tbsp blue cheese butter

Preparation Method

1. Use package directions to prepare blue cheese butter.
2. Remove steaks from the fridge just 15 minutes before recipe stars.
3. Preheat your air fryer to 400°F for at least 5 minutes.
4. Meanwhile, coat steak sides completely with garlic powder, salt and pepper pressing with your hands.
5. Place steaks in the air fryer basket then close.
6. Cook for about 4 minutes at 400°F then flip and cook for another 3 minutes. Turn off your fryer but don't open and sit for a minute.
7. Top with cheese and serve. Enjoy!

Nutritional Information

Calories: 829, Total fat: 60g, Saturated fat: 29g, Total carbs: 2g, Net carbs: 2g, Protein: 69g, Sugar: 0g, Fiber: 0g, Sodium: 2602mg, Potassium: 949mg

Air Fryer Beef And Broccoli

Looking for a quick healthy meal? Air Fryer beef and broccoli is quick, easy, healthy, and full of flavor especially Asian flavor. Kids will absolutely love this meal when broccoli cooks in mini pieces.

Prep time: 1 hour, **Cook time**: 15 minutes; **Serves** 3

Ingredients

½ lb round steak, strips cut

1 lb broccoli florets

⅓ cup oyster sauce

2 tbsp soy sauce

2 tbsp sesame oil

1 tbsp ginger, minced

1 tbsp garlic, minced

Preparation Method

1. Mix all ingredients in a bowl, medium, and let sit for about 1 hour to marinate.
2. Place everything in an air fryer basket and cook for about 12-15 minutes at 350ₒF. Shake severally.
3. Serve over rice.
4. Enjoy!

Nutritional Information

Calories: 263, Total Fat: 14g, Saturated fat: 2g, Total carbs: 13g, Net carbs: 10g, Protein: 22g, Sugar: 2g, Fiber: 3g, Sodium: 1347mg, Potassium: 778mg

Air Fryer Orange Beef

This orange beef tastes good perfect for a weeknight dinner. Cornstarch gives this recipe an extra crispy coating when prepared in an air fryer. The meal is amazing and does not disappoint that you will absolutely enjoyed together with your family.

Prep time: 10 minutes, **Cook time:** 20 minutes; **Serves** 4

Ingredients

1 tbsp sesame oil

1 red pepper, sliced

1 yellow pepper, sliced

1 orange pepper, sliced

½ cup soy sauce

¾ cup sugar

½ cup orange juice

1 tbsp orange zest

½ tbsp minced garlic

½ tbsp ground ginger

1- 1½ lbs sirloin steak, Certified Angus Beef brand

¼ cup cornstarch

¼ tbsp salt

¼ tbsp pepper

Optional: sesame seeds and rice or cauliflower

Preparation Method

1. Heat oil in a large skillet over high-medium heat then add all peppers and cook until tender. Now reduce the heat to low.
2. Add soy sauce, orange zest, orange juice, ginger, sugar, and garlic in a saucepan. Whisk together to combine.
3. Boil and simmer for about 10 minutes over medium-low heat until ready. Add ½ tbsp cornstarch if runny and thin.
4. Meanwhile, slice the steak into thin slices.
5. Add pepper and salt to cornstarch mixture then toss the steak slices.
6. Spray your fryer basket with non-stick cooking spray then add steak slices.
7. Cook for about 10 minutes at 350°F then flip and cook for another 5 minutes until crispy and to desired doneness.
8. Remove and place over peppers in the skillet then add the sauce. Stir to coat.
9. Place sesame seeds on top and serve warm over rice or cauliflower.
10. Enjoy!

Nutritional Information

Calories: 274, Total fat: 4.1g, Saturated fat: 2g, Total carbs: 55.9g, Net carbs: 45.9g, Protein: 5.7g, Sugar: 41.8g, Fiber: 10g, Sodium: 1299mg, Potassium: 981mg

Air Fryer Pork Loin

Air Fryer Pork Loin turns out as soft and tasty on the inside, and enjoyable and browned on the outside! Air Fryer Pork Loin is quick to prepare and just take just takes a total of 20 minutes to cook. If you are planning to consume healthier meals for the New Year, this recipe is for you!

Prep time: 2 minutes, cook time: 22 minutes; Serves 6

Ingredients

1 ½ lb pork loin, dried

Nonstick cooking spray

Salt and pepper to taste

2 tbsp garlic scape pesto

Preparation Method

1. Thinly coat pork loin with non-stick cooking spray.
2. Add salt, pepper and garlic scape pesto.
3. Apply cooking spray on air fryer tray.
4. Preheat your air fryer to 400 ·F. Arrange pork loin and cook for 8-10 minutes then remove and flip over and cook further for 8-10 minutes.
5. Serve warm.

Nutritional Information

Calories 338, Total Fat: 10g, Saturated Fat: 3g, Total Carbs: 0g, Net Carbs: 0g, Protein: 62g, Sugar: 0g, Fiber: 0g, Sodium: 157mg, Potassium: 1188mg

Frozen Chicken Breast in an Air fryer

Do you always forget to defrost your chicken but have a few minutes to make dinner? I forget all the time. The air fryer cooks this frozen chicken breast perfectly; you do not have to thaw your chicken. A brilliant hack. right?

Prep time: 5 minutes, **Cook time**: 15 minutes; **Serves**: 2

Ingredients

2 chicken breasts, frozen

½ tbsp salt

¼ tbsp pepper

¼ tbsp garlic powder

¼ tbsp parsley flakes

Preparation Method

1. Place chicken breasts in the air fryer then sprinkle all ingredients evenly on top and between them.
2. Close air fryer and cook at 360∘F for 15 minutes.
3. Allow the chicken to sit before slicing them. Serve and enjoy.

Nutritional Information

Calories 260, Total Fat 6g, Saturated Fat 1g, Total Carbs 1g, Net Carbs 1g, Protein 48g, sugar 1g Sodium 844mg, Potassium 836mg

Ninja Foodi chicken Tenders

Air fryer chicken tenders wrapped in bacon are the bomb. Of cos, plain chicken tenders make a great dinner but trust me wrapped chicken tenders are irresistible. They are healthy, crispy and filling dinner that even your kids will love. Serve the chicken tenders with baked macaroni and cheese for a complete meal.

Prep time: 15 minutes, **Cook time**: 12 minutes; **Serves**:5

Ingredients

1 egg whisked

½ cup bread crumbs

2 tbsp olive oil

1 lb chicken tenders

8 slices bacon, halved

Preparation Method

1. Whip the egg in a mixing bowl.
2. In a mixing bowl, mix bread crumbs with olive oil.
3. Preheat your air fryer to 350ₒF for 10 minutes.
4. Dip chicken tenders in egg then in bread crumbs mixture each at a time.
5. Lay 2 bacon pieces horizontally next to one other. Place the coated chicken tenders in the middle then wrap with bacon. Use toothpicks to secure the ends.
6. Place the wrapped chicken pieces in the air fryer without overlapping, close the lid and cook for 14 minutes.Flic the tender halfway through the cooking time.
7. Serve and enjoy.

Nutritional Information

Calories 443, Total Fat 29g, Saturated Fat 7g, Total Carbs 10g, Net Carbs 10g, Protein 32g, Sodium 537mg, Potassium 548mg

Air fryer Chicken Kabobs

Are you obsessed with easy recipes while keeping it healthy? Chicken kabobs are healthier fast food to serve for dinner or appetizer to your loved ones. They are packed with veggies and low in fat. These kabobs are easy and quick to make and have you get crispy outside without using any oil.

Prep time: 15 minutes, **Cook time**: 18 minutes; **Serves**:6

Ingredients

1 garlic clove, minced

1 lemon, juiced

¼ cup olive oil

2 tbsp red wine vinegar

1 tbsp oregano

2 chicken breasts, diced

1 zucchini, sliced lengthwise

1 yellow onion, cut into bite-size pieces

1 ½ cup grape tomatoes

1 tbsp olive oil

Preparation Method

1. In a mixing bowl, whisk together garlic, lemon juice, ¼ cup olive oil, and wine vinegar. Add chicken pieces in the mixture and allow to marinate for 30 minutes.
2. Make sure the skewers will fit in your air fryer then put the chicken alternating with the vegetables.
3. Place the kabobs in the air fryer and close the lid.
4. Cook at 380◦F for 16 minutes or until the chicken is cooked through

Nutritional Information

Calories 354, Total Fat 17.7g, Saturated Fat 3g, Total Carbs 22.5g, Net Carbs 20g, Protein 26.9g, Sugar 2g, Fiber 2.5g, Sodium 309mg, Potassium 415mg

Air fryer Chicken Thighs

What I love about these chicken thighs is that they are cheap, deliciously crispy outer skin, tender and moist in the inside. They are above all easy and quick to prepare. The secret for perfect wings is flipping them halfway through the cooking time for even cooking.

Prep time: 10 minutes, **Cook time**: 25 minutes; **Serves**:4

Ingredients

4 chicken thighs, bone and skin on

2 tbsp salt

¼ tbsp brown sugar

¼ tbsp paprika

2 tbsp garlic powder

½ tbsp chili powder

2 tbsp olive oil

Preparation Method

1. Mix all ingredients in a mixing bowl.
2. Preheat your air fryer to 375₀F for 5 minutes.
3. Rub oil on each of the chicken thighs then rub the spices on all sides of thighs. Press the thighs so that the spices stick.
4. Arrange the chicken thighs on a trivet that has been sprayed with oil
5. Place the thighs in the air fryer and cook for 15 minutes. Flip and cook for 12 more minutes.
6. Serve and enjoy.

Nutritional Information

Calories 368, Total Fat 25g, Saturated Fat 6g, Total Carbs 15g, Net Carbs 15g, Protein 18g, Sugar 13g, Fiber 0g, Sodium 1260mg, Potassium 268mg

Crispy Parmesan Buttermilk Chicken Tenders

Whether you are a lover of chicken strips, chicken tenders chicken nuggets or chicken fine greatest question has always been who prepares the best. Air fryer gives you the best; juicy crispy chicken tenders without deep frying. Fairly simple, kids and adult approved meal.

Prep time: 10 minutes, **Cook time**: 18 minutes; **Serves**:4

Ingredients

¾ cup buttermilk

1 ½ tbsp Worcestershire sauce, divided

¾ tbsp kosher salt

¾ tbsp black pepper, freshly ground

½ tbsp smoked paprika, divided

2 chicken breast, boneless and skinless

2 tbsp butter

1 ½ cup panko breadcrumbs

¼ cup parmesan cheese

2 eggs

½ cup all-purpose flour

Honey mustard sauce

Preparation Method

1. In a mixing bowl, mix buttermilk, half Worcestershire sauce, half salt, half pepper, and half paprika. Add the mixture in a gallon freezer bag with the chicken.
2. Refrigerate for 6 hours or overnight.
3. Melt butter in a saucepan until it foams. Mix butter with bread crumbs until well combined. Add cheese and mix well to combine.
4. Whisk eggs in a mixing bowl with the remaining Worcestershire sauce.
5. In a separate bowl mix flour, remaining salt, pepper, and paprika.
6. Drain the chicken and discard buttermilk. Use tongs to dip the chicken in flour, then in the egg and finally in the bread crumbs.
7. Preheat the air fryer to 400₀F then place the chicken tenders without overlapping them.

8. Cook for 15 minutes flipping chicken halfway through cooking time. Repeat with the remaining tenders.
9. Serve and enjoy.

Nutritional Information

Calories 350, Total Fat 14g, Saturated Fat 7g, Total Carbs 32g, Net Carbs 30g, Protein 23g, Sugar 4g, Fiber 2g, Sodium 913mg, Potassium 379mg

Air Fryer Turkey Breast

The turkey breast comes out juicy and moist with deep golden brown crispy skin. If looking for a thanksgiving meal, this turkey breast is perfect. moreover, this turkey breast cooks in a fraction of the time it would have cooked in the oven.

Prep time: 5 minutes, **Cook time**: 55 minutes; **Serves**:10

Ingredients

4 lb turkey breast, bone, and skin on

1 tbsp olive oil

2 tbsp kosher salt

½ tbsp turkey seasoning

Preparation Method

1. Rub half of the olive oil on the turkey breast then season with kosher salt and turkey seasoning.
2. Preheat the air fryer to 350°F and cook the turkey breast skin down for 20 minutes.
3. Let it rest for 10 minutes before serving.
4. Enjoy.

Nutritional Information

Calories 226, Total Fat 10g, Saturated Fat 2.5g, Protein 32.5g, Sodium 296mg

Tandoori Chicken

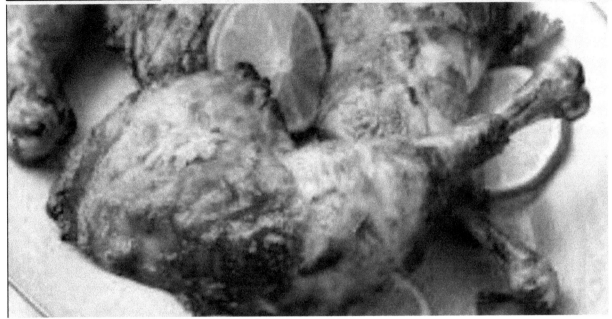

Apart from being the cheapest and easiest way to introduce Indian food, tandoori chicken is prepared by marinating chicken in a yogurt marinade. It is thereafter spiced up with cayenne pepper, turmeric, and garam masala, Serve the chicken alone as an appetizer or serve with raita dip, green chutney or in lettuce leaves as a wrap.

Prep time: 30 minutes, **Cook time**: 15 minutes; **Serves**:4

Ingredients

1 lb chicken tenders

¼ cup greek yogurt

1 tbsp ginger, minced

1 tbsp garlic, minced

¼ cup cilantro

1 tbsp salt

½ - 1 tbsp cayenne

1 tbsp turmeric

1 tbsp garam masala

1 tbsp smoked paprika

For Finishing

1 tbsp oil

2 tbsp lemon juice

2 tbsp cilantro

Preparation Method

1. Mix all ingredients in a mixing bowl except the finishing ingredients.
2. Let the chicken breast marinate for 30 minutes.
3. Lay the chicken tandoori in the air fryer in a single layer then baste the chicken with oil.
4. Cook at 350◦F for 10 minutes. Flip the chicken and baste on the other side.
5. Cook for 5 more minutes. Remove the chicken tandoori form the air fryer and place on a serving plate. Add lemon juice then sprinkle with cilantro. Enjoy.

Nutritional Information

Calories 178, Total Fat 6g, Saturated Fat 1g, Total Carbs 2g, Protein 25g

Air fried General Tso's Chicken

This general Tso's chicken saves the day and has almost a have of saturated fats in the restaurant general Tso's chicken. If you have a small size air fryer cook these Tso chicken in batches to give room for air circulation to crisp up the chicken.

Prep time: 20 minutes, **Cook time**: 15 minutes; **Serves**:4

Ingredients

1 egg

⅓ cup + 2 tbsp cornstarch

¼ tbsp kosher salt

¼ tbsp white pepper, ground

1 lb chicken thighs, boneless and skinless

7 tbsp chicken broth, low sodium

2 tbsp soy sauce, low sodium

2 tbsp sugar

2 tbsp ketchup

2 tbsp rice vinegar, unseasoned

1 ½ tbsp canola oil

4 chiles de arbol, chopped and seeds discarded

1 tbsp fresh ginger, chopped

2 tbsp green onion, thinly sliced and divided

1 tbsp sesame oil, toasted

½ tbsp sesame seeds, toasted

Preparation Method

1. Beat an egg in a mixing bowl then add chicken. Mix to coat well.
2. In a separate bowl, mix ⅓ tbsp cornstarch, salt, and pepper. Transfer the chicken to the cornstarch mixture then mix until well coated.
3. Transfer the coated chicken to the air fryer oven rack without overlapping.
4. Preheat the air fryer at 400°F for 3 minutes.
5. Cook the chicken for 15 minutes.
6. Meanwhile, whisk remaining cornstarch with chicken broth, soy sauce, sugar, ketchup, and vinegar.
7. Heat oil and chiles in a skillet over medium heat. Add ginger and garlic when the starts to sizzle.
8. Re whisk cornstarch mixture then stir into the skillet. When the sauce bubbles add chicken and stir well to evenly coat.
9. Cook until the sauce thickens. Turn off the heat then add green onions and sesame oil.
10. Serve and top with sesame seeds. Enjoy.

Nutritional Information

Calories 302, Total Fat 13g, Saturated Fat 3g, Total Carbs 18g, Net Carbs 18g, Protein 26g, Sugar 4g, Fiber 0g, Sodium 611mg

Air Fryer Chicken Nuggets

If a lover of chicken nuggets, you can now make your own at home. Just take your chicken breast chunks, coat with cheese and breadcrumbs, air fry until crisp and golden brown in your air fryer. Simple right? You now don't have to visit the restaurant for nuggets.

Prep time: 10 minutes, **Cook time**: 10 minutes; **Serves**: 4

Ingredients

2 tbsp olive oil

6 tbsp Italian seasoned breadcrumbs, whole wheat

2 tbsp panko

2 tbsp parmesan cheese, grated

16 oz chicken breast, boneless and skinless

½ tbsp kosher salt and black pepper

Olive oil spray

Preparation Method

1. Preheat your air fryer to 400°F for 8 minutes.
2. Put olive oil in a mixing bowl.
3. In a separate bowl, mix bread crumbs, panko, and cheese.
4. Season chicken breasts with salt and pepper then put in the bowl with olive oil. Coat well.
5. Put the chicken in the bowl with breadcrumbs mixture, coat well then transfer to the air fryer basket.
6. Spray with olive oil then fry for 8 minutes turning halfway through the cooking period.
7. Serve and enjoy.

Nutritional Information

Calories 188, Total Fat 4.5g, Saturated Fat 1g, Total Carbs 8g, Net Carbs 8g, Protein 25g, Sugar 0.5g, Fiber 0g, Sodium 427mg

Chicken Chimichangas

Anytime you have leftover chicken, chicken chimichangas are the best to prepare with the leftovers. You can, however, make your own shredded chicken in the slow cooker. These chicken chimichangas can be served with p=
Pico de gallo, sour cream and avocado for a complete and filling meal.

Prep time: 15 minutes, **Cook time**: 20 minutes; **Serves**: 4

Ingredients

The Pico de Gallo

½ cup tomato, diced

3 tbsp onion, chopped

1 tbsp fresh cilantro, plus more for garnish

1 tbsp lime juice

¼ tbsp kosher salt

Black pepper, freshly ground

The chimichangas

12 oz chicken breast, shredded

½ navel orange juice

½ lime juice

1 garlic clove, minced

1 tbsp cumin, ground

4 oz green chiles, diced

4 wheat tortillas

½ cup jack cheese, shredded

Olive oil spray

3 cups lettuce, shredded

4 tbsp sour cream

4 oz avocado, diced

Preparation Method

For the pico de gallo

1. In a small mixing bowl, mix all pico de gallo ingredients.

For the chimichangas

1. In a mixing bowl, mix chicken breast, orange and lime juice, garlic clove, cumin, and green chiles.
2. Place a quarter of the chicken breast mixture on the bottom third of a tortilla, sprinkle with 2 tablespoons cheese then wrap the tortilla around the filling.
3. Set aside with the seam side down. Repeat with all the mixture and tortillas.
4. Preheat the air fryer to 400°F.
5. Spray the tortillas with oil on all sides and place two of them in the air fryer basket seam side down.
6. Cook for 8 minutes flipping halfway through the cooking time.
7. Repeat the prosses with the remaining chimichangas.
8. Place ¾ cup of shredded lettuce on a plate, place 1 chimichanga, 2 tablespoon pico de gallo, 1 tablespoon sour cream and 1 oz avocado. Enjoy.

Nutritional Information

Calories 391, Total Fat 18.5g, Saturated Fat 6g, Total Carbs 30g, Net Carbs 13.5g, Protein 40g, Sugar 5g, Fiber 16.5g, Sodium 716mg

Chicken Parmesan in the Air fryer

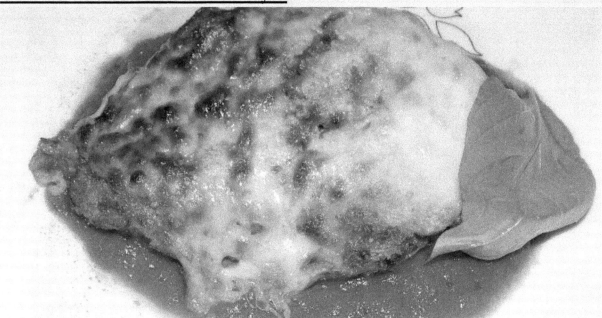

Chicken parmesan comes out more crispy and delicious in the air fryer than in an oven. It a quick and simple dinner that every member of your family will love. Serve this chicken parmesan with vegetables for a complete dinner dish and to win over everyone

Prep time: 10 minutes, **Cook time**: 12 minutes; **Serves**:5

Ingredients

6 tbsp breadcrumbs

2 tbsp parmesan cheese, grated

1 tbsp butter, melted

16 oz chicken breast, sliced in half

6 tbsp mozzarella cheese, reduced fat

½ cup marinara

Cooking spray

Preparation Method

1. Preheat your air fryer to 360°F for 3 minutes.
2. Combine breadcrumbs with cheese in a mixing bowl.
3. Brush butter on the chicken then dip it in the breadcrumb mixture..
4. Place 2 pieces of chicken in the air fryer then spray oil.
5. After the chicken has cooked for 6 minutes, flip it then top each with 1 tbsp marinara sauce and 1 ½ tbsp mozzarella cheese.
6. Cook for 3 minutes or until the cheese has melted.
7. Repeat the process with the remaining chicken pieces.
8. Serve and enjoy.

Nutritional Information

Calories 251, Total Fat 9.5g, Saturated Fat 3.5g, Total Carbs 14g, Net Carbs 12.5g, Protein 31.5g, Fiber 1.5g, Sodium 829mg

Ninja Foodi Garlic and Parm Crusted Chicken with Roasted Potatoes

I have an incredible lunch or dinner idea for you or for your family gathering. It's an easy, savory, and filling dish that is a real crowd-pleaser. The garlic and parmesan keeps the chicken inside moist as it bakes and crunchy on the outside. The leftovers can be preserved in the fridge for up to 3 days

Prep time: 10 minutes, **Cook time**: 12 minutes; **Serves**:5

Ingredients

1 tbsp Italian seasonings

1 tbsp garlic powder

5 lb potatoes, cubed

1 ½ sticks butter, melted

1 cup panko bread crumbs

½ cup parmesan cheese, shredded

1 egg, whisked

1 lb chicken breast

½ tbsp salt

½ tbsp pepper

Preparation Method

1. Mix Italian seasonings with garlic powder in a mixing bowl.
2. Place potatoes at the bottom of your air fryer then pour over butter ensuring they are well coated. Mix bread crumbs with cheese in a mixing bowl.
3. Rub the chicken with the spice mix.
4. Dip the chicken breast in egg then into bread crumbs mixture.
5. Place a trivet in the air fryer over the potatoes then place the chicken on the trivet.
6. Cook on manual for 10 minutes at high pressure. Do a quick pressure release.
7. Remove the lid and cook on the air fryer at 390°F for 15 minutes. Serve and enjoy.

Nutritional Information

Calories 805, Total Fat 30g, Saturated Fat 17g, Total Carbs 96g, Net Carbs 86g, Protein 39g, Sugar 6g, Fiber 10g, Sodium 1099mg

Zesty Ranch Air Fryer Fish Fillets

Have you just got your air fryer? If so, I know you are in search of delicious new recipes to make in it. Trust me this zesty ranch fish fillet is among the best recipes you will make in your new air fryer.

Prep time: 5 minutes, **Cook time**: 12 minutes; **Serves**:4

Ingredients

¾ cup bread crumbs

130g ranch-style dressing mix

2 ½ tbsp vegetable oil

4 tilapia fillets or other fish

2 egg, beaten

lemon wedges for garnish

Preparation Method

1. Preheat your air fryer to 356°F.
2. Mix bread crumb and ranch dressing in a mixing bowl. Add vegetable oil into the bread crumb mixture.
3. Stir the mixture until crumbly and loose.
4. Dip the fish in egg then in the bread crumb mixture.
5. Place them in the air fryer for 13 minutes.
6. Remove the fillet from the air fryer and serve. Squeeze lemon wedges over fish and enjoy.

Nutritional Information

Calories 315, Total Fat 14g, Saturated Fat 8g, Total Carbs 8g, Net Carbs 8g, Protein 38g, Fiber 1g, Sodium 220mg, Potassium 565mg

Air fryer Tilapia

Are you a lover of fish? Me too!! The first time I tried air fryer tilapia it came out even better than I expected. I could eat it every night for dinner if I could. Feel free to use either fresh or frozen fish because the end results will always be a tasty dish that's crunchy on the outside and flaky on the inside.

Prep time: 15 minutes, **Cook time**: 5 minutes; **Serves**:5

Ingredients

4 fish fillets

1 cup Italian bread crumbs

1 egg, whisked

1 ½ tbsp Old Bay

Olive oil

Preparation Method

1. Preheat air fryer to 400◦F.
2. Mix bread crumbs with seasoning in a mixing bowl.
3. Dip the fish in egg then in bread crumbs mixture then place the fillet in the air fryer basket.
4. Repeat with all fish fillets without overlapping them.
5. Close the lid and cook for 6 minutes.
6. Serve and enjoy

Nutritional Information

Calories 109, Total Fat 2g, Saturated Fat 1g, Total Carbs 17g, Net Carbs 16g, Protein 5g, Sugar 1g, Fiber 1g, Sodium 334mg, Potassium 77mg

Air Fryer Herbed Salmon

There is nothing cheap like making salmon in the air fryer. Jus less than 10 minutes and it's ready on your dining table. If you love an easy and quick and healthy meal, then this recipe is ideal for you.

Prep time: 1 minute, **Cook time**: 5 minutes; **Serves**:2

Ingredients

8 oz fish salmon fillets

2 tbsp olive oil

1 tbsp Herbs de Provence

¼ tbsp salt

¼ tbsp black pepper

¼ tbsp smoked paprika

1 tbsp Medlee Seasoned Butter, melted

Preparation Method

1. Pat your fish fillets dry with paper towel then gently run the surface to ensure there are no bones.
2. Drizzle the fish fillet with oil on all sides.
3. Mix the seasonings and sprinkle on both sides of the fillet.
4. Turn your air fryer to 390°F and cook the fillets for 8 minutes.
5. Serve the fish and pour over the butter before eating

Nutritional Information

Calories 338, Total Fat 27g, Saturated Fat 7g, Total Carbs 1g, Net Carbs 0g, Protein 23g, Sugar 1g, Fiber 1g, Sodium 392mg, Potassium 556mg

Air Fried Crumbed Fish

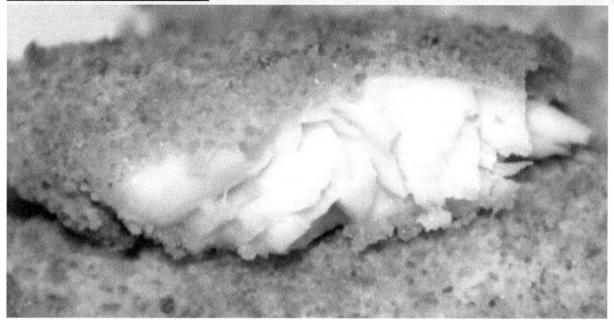

This is my best version of crumbled fish. It's packed with flavor and very low in fat making it super healthy. The good news is that you can use the type of fish you desire plus ten minutes meal is all you need during those busy lunch breaks or tight dinners.

Prep time: 10 minutes, **Cook time**: 12 minutes; **Serves**:5

Ingredients

1 cup bread crumbs

¼ cup vegetable oil

4 flounder fillets

1 egg, beaten

1 lemon, sliced

Preparation Method

1. Preheat your Air fryer to 350ᵒF.
2. Mix bread crumbs with vegetable oil in a mixing bowl until the mixture is crumbly.
3. Dip the fish fillet in beaten egg then dip in bread crumbs mixture and coat evenly.
4. Lay the fillets in the air fryer and cook for 12 minutes or until fish flakes easily with a spoon.
5. Garnish with lemon slices and enjoy.

Nutritional Information

Calories 354, Total Fat 17.7g, Saturated Fat 3g, Total Carbs 22.5g, Net Carbs 20g, Protein 26.9g, Sugar 2g, Fiber 2.5g, Sodium 309mg, Potassium 415mg

Air Fryer Southern Style Catfish With Green Beans

Nothing beats this hearty meal prepared in an air fryer. It is an easy recipe to make as it takes les than 30 minutes to prepare, it is crispy and delicious fish fillet that you will fall in love with.

Prep time: 10 minutes, **Cook time**: 25 minutes; **Serves** 2

Ingredients

12 oz trimmed green beans, fresh

Cooking spray

1 tbsp light brown sugar

Optional: ½ tbsp red pepper, crushed

⅜ tbsp divided kosher salt

6 oz catfish fillets

¼ cup all-purpose flour

1 lightly-beaten egg, large

⅓ cup panko

¼ tbsp black pepper

2 tbsp mayonnaise

1½ tbsp fresh dill, finely chopped

¾ tbsp dill pickle relish

½ tbsp apple cider vinegar

⅛ tbsp granulated sugar

Lemon wedges

Preparation Method

1. Place beans in a bowl, medium, and spray using cooking spray then splash with red pepper, sugar, and ⅛ tbsp salt.
2. Place in a fryer basket then cook for about 12 minutes at 400◦F until tender and browned. Transfer to medium bowl to cover to keep warm, use aluminum foil to cover.
3. In the meantime, coat catfish with flour and shake to drip off excess then dip in egg for a coating. Splash with panko to evenly coat on all sides.
4. Place catfish in your fryer basket and cook for about 8 minutes at 400◦F until cooked through and browned. Splash with remaining salt and pepper.
5. Meanwhile, whisk together, dill, mayonnaise, relish, sugar, and vinegar in a bowl, small.
6. Serve green beans and fish with lemon wedges and the sauce.
7. Enjoy!

Nutritional Information

Calories: 416, Total fat: 18g, Saturated fat: 3.5g, Total carbs: 31g, Net carbs: 24g, Protein: 33g, Sugar: 8g, Fiber: 7g, Sodium: 677mg, Potassium: 509mg

Roasted Salmon With Fennel Salad

Air frying is a perfect method for preparing or roasting fish fillets and everything comes out easily. If you need to add an extra half, serve this dish with your favorite brown rice. Try and enjoy a fantastic dinner for two.

Prep time: 15 minutes, **Cook time**: 10 minutes; **Serves** 4

Ingredients

2 tbsp flat-leaf parsley, finely-chopped and fresh

1 tbsp fresh thyme, finely chopped

1 tbsp divided kosher salt

4, 6 oz, salmon fillets, center-cut and skinless

2 tbsp olive oil

4 cups fennel, thinly sliced

⅔ cup Greek yogurt, reduced-fat

1 grated garlic clove

2 tbsp orange juice, fresh

1 tbsp lemon juice, fresh

2 tbsp fresh dill, chopped

Preparation Method

1. Preheat an oven to 200°F.
2. Combine thyme, ½ tbsp salt, and parsley in a bowl, small, then brush salmon with olive oil and splash with the mixture.
3. Place salmon in your fryer basket, 2 at a time, and cook for about 10 minutes at 350°F until the desired doneness. Repeat for the remaining fish fillets.
4. Meanwhile, toss together yogurt, fennel, orange juice, garlic, lemon juice, remaining salt, and dill in a bowl, medium. Serve salmon with fennel salad. Enjoy!

Nutritional Information

Calories: 464, Total Fat: 30g, Saturated fat: 7g, Total carbs: 9g, Net carbs: 6g, Protein: 38g, Sugar: 5g, Fiber: 3g, Sodium: 635mg, Potassium: 540mg

Fish And Chips

Spiralized potato fries gives this recipe an extra-crispy factor that everyone will love and can not be found in any grocery store. The air fryer recipe has added flavor which is brought by the malt vinegar with no calories added. You will like it trust me.

Prep time: 15 minutes, **Cook time**: 30 minutes; **Serves** 4

Ingredients

2, 10 oz, scrubbed russet potatoes

Cooking spray

1¼ tbsp divided kosher salt

1 cup all-purpose flour

2 eggs, large

2 tbsp water

1 cup panko, whole-wheat

4, 6 oz, tilapia fillets, skinless

½ cup malt vinegar

Preparation Method

1. Use package instructions to spiralize potatoes to spirals.
2. Place potatoes spirals in batches in your air fryer basket then spray coating completely with cooking spray.
3. Cook for about 10 minutes at 375◦F until crispy and golden brown. Turn halfway.
4. Remove, evenly splash with ¼ tbsp salt and keep warm.
5. Meanwhile, combine ½ tbsp salt and flour in a dish, shallow.

6. Whisk together water and eggs in another dish, shallow, then in a third dish, shallow, stir together remaining salt and panko.
7. Cut lengthwise each fillet into long strips, 2, then dip in four mixture. Shake off excess.
8. Dip the fillet strips into egg mixture and in panko mixture. Drip off excess on each.
9. Spray cooking spray on both sides of the fillet to coat. Layer in a fryer basket and cook for about 10 minutes at 375°F until golden brown. Turn halfway.
10. Divide fish fillets among 4 plates and equal potato spirals portions then place 2 tbsp malt vinegar on each plate for dipping.
11. Serve and enjoy!

Nutritional Information

Calories: 415, Total fat: 7g, Saturated fat: 2g, Total carbs: 46g, Net carbs: 42g, Protein: 44g, Sugar: 2g, Fiber: 4g, Sodium: 754mg, Potassium: 636mg

Air Fryer Lemon Pepper Shrimp

These shrimp are easy to make, can be served with salad and are great served as a cold appetizer. This recipe comes out perfectly when prepared in an air fryer a well as having a great flavor. Everyone including your kids will love it.

Prep time: 5 minutes, **Cook time**: 10 minutes; **Serves** 2

Ingredients

1 tbsp olive oil

1 juiced lemon

1 tbsp lemon pepper

¼ tbsp paprika

¼ tbsp garlic powder

12 oz peeled and deveined medium shrimp, uncooked

1 sliced lemon

Preparation Method

1. Preheat your air fryer to 200◦C or 400◦F.
2. Combine olive oil, lemon pepper, lemon juice, garlic powder, and paprika in a medium bowl.
3. Add and toss shrimp in the mixture until well coated.
4. Place coated shrimp into your air fryer and cook for about 6-8 minutes until punk.
5. Serve alongside lemon slices.
6. Enjoy!

Nutritional Information

Calories: 215, Total Fat: 8.6g, Saturated fat: 1g, Total carbs: 12.6g, Net carbs: 7.1g, Protein: 28.9g, Sugar: 0g, Fiber: 5.5g, Sodium: 52mg, Potassium: 414mg

Air-fryer Fish Sticks

Air-Fryer Fish Sticks are great cuisine that we all hate to avoid! This version of the dish is prepared in air-fryer and from a short list of ingredients and includes the sweet side tartar sauce. They're family-friendly and rewarm easily so one can prepare considerable amount for quick luncheon or supper anytime in just 30 minutes!

Prep time: 10 minutes, **Cook time**: 30 minutes, **Serves**: 2

Ingredients

1- 1 ½ lb white fish

½ cup tapioca starch

2 eggs

1 tbsp ground black pepper

1 tbsp fine sea salt

½ tbsp mustard powder

1 ½ tbsp dill, dried,

1 ½ tbsp onion powder

1 cup almond flour

2 tbsp avocado oil

Avocado oil, spray,

Preparation Method

1. Preheat your air fryer up to 390 degrees.
2. Tap white fish dry with a paper towel then season with pepper and salt.
3. Slice your fish into small sticks about ½ x ½ x 2 inches.

4. Place tapioca starch in a medium bowl, then whisk eggs in another bowl.
5. Whisk pepper, salt, mustard powder, dill, onion powder and almond flour in a large bowl.
6. Pour in fish slices into tapioca shaking off any excess and then into the eggs.
7. Scoop in flour mixture and repeat to make sure the fish is all coated and add avocado oil to the basket.
8. Spray generously the basket of the air fryer with the avocado spray then place spacing as many fish sticks as possible.
9. Spray the remaining avocado spray over the fish stick to lightly coat.
10. Fry for 11 minutes, and turn over delicately once at 5 minutes.
11. To make tartar sauce mix all ingredients in a bowl then set aside.
12. Repeat the process with the remaining fish until all have been cooked to a temperature of 145 degrees, don't overcook or fish will fall apart.
13. Serve warm with tartar sauce or completely cool before you freeze.

Nutritional information

Calories: 598, Total Fat: 22.5g, Saturated fat: 3.3g, Total carbs: 33.2g, Net carbs: 30.3g, Protein: 61.7g, Sugar: 1.1g, Fiber: 2.9g, Sodium: 1600mg

Air Fryer Tuna Patties

Air Fryer Tuna Patties is a great meal that is fit for a king! This dish is such a hit! And much healthier since it barely uses any oil. The air fried type is a bit drier compared to stovetop variety, but this kind is still classic and sweet. Slight differences in taste and texture exist between pan-fried tuna version and air fried tuna version. Making tuna patties in an air fryer is certainly the way if you want to cut calories and use less oil.

Prep time: 15 minutes, **Cook time:** 10 minutes, **Serves** 10

Ingredients

1 lb freshly diced tuna or 15 oz canned albacore tuna

1 medium zest lemon

1 tbsp lemon juice

2-3 eggs

3 tbsp parmesan cheese, grated,

½ cup bread crumbs

½ tbsp garlic powder

3 tbsp minced onions

1 stalk finely chopped celery

¼ tbsp kosher salt

½ tbsp dried herbs

Black pepper, fresh cracked,

Optional, Tartar sauce, mayo, lemon slices

Preparation Method

1. In a large bowl mix together lemon zest, lemon juice, eggs, parmesan cheese, bread crumbs, garlic powder, onions, celery, salt, dried herbs, and pepper stir the mixture well to combine.
2. To combine, gentle Fold in the tuna.
3. Use liner or perforated baking paper and lay it inside the base of air fryer then spray olive oil to prevent patties from sticking.
4. Scoop ¼ cup of mixture and shape to make about 10 patties of about 3" wide and ½ " thick then lay them in your basket.
5. To make your patties easier to handle when cooking, chill them until firm, about 1 hour.
6. Spray oil on the tops of your patties then cook in your air fryer for 10 minutes on 360 degrees and flip after 5 minutes.,
7. Spray with oil again after flipping.
8. Serve with lemon slices and sauce of choice.

Nutritional information

Calories: 387, Total Fat: 17g, Saturated fat: 7g, Total carbs: 21g, Net carbs: 19g, Protein: 38g, Sugar: 4g, Fiber: 2g, Sodium: 1007mg, Potassium 460mg

Air Fryer Lemon Garlic Salmon

This is not your typical underrated salmon fish! For a fact, considering it features not only salmon filets but also garlic, pepper, lemon, and Italian herbs. Its crispy, soft, flavorful and perfectly cooked and furthermore it only cooks under 17 minutes. The unique flavor of this dish will leave you bowled over and addicted to it.

Prep time: 5 minutes, **cook time**: 17 minutes; **Serves** 4

Ingredients

4.6 oz salmon filets.

1 tbsp lemon juice

2 tbsp olive oil

2 tbsp garlic powder

Salt and pepper to taste

1 lemon, thinly sliced

2 tbsp Italian herbs

Preparation Method

1. Coat the salmon fillets with lemon juice and olive oil.
2. Spice with garlic, salt, pepper, and Italian herbs.
3. Arrange salmon fillets in air fryer basket and spread lemon slices over them.
4. Preheat your air fryer to 400 ·F cook the salmon fillet for 12 minutes.
5. Serve warm.

Nutritional information

Calories 460, Total Fat: 28g, Saturated Fat: 5g, Total Carbs: 13g, Net Carbs: 11g, Protein: 39g, Sugar: 8g, Fiber: 2g, Sodium: 724, Potassium: 0mg

Coconut Shrimp

Air-fried coconut shrimp has an amazing crispy, tangy-sweet aroma and its addictive appearance will make you feel that you're on a Caribbean Beach! This dish is easy and quick to prepare and it will just take a total of 30 minutes to cook. Once you familiarize yourself with this dish you will always feel motivated preparing it.

Prep time: 15 minutes, **cook time**: 30 minutes; **Serves** 4

Ingredients

½ cup flour

1 ½ tbsp pepper

12 oz shrimp, medium peeled, deveined and tail-on

2 large eggs, whisked

⅔ cup coconut, unsweetened and flaked

⅓ cup panko

Cooking spray

Salt to taste

¼ cup honey

¼ cup lime juice

1 serrano chile, thinly sliced

Preparation Method

1. Stir flour and pepper in a mixing bowl. Mix coconut and panko in a separate dish.
2. Holding the shrimp by the tail dip it in flour mixture, then dip it in whisked eggs and finally dip in coconut mixture then coat with cooking spray.
3. Preheat your air fryer to 400 F. Arrange the shrimp and air fry for 6-8 minutes and add salt.
4. As shrimp cook, whip together honey, lime juice, and serrano chile in a small bowl.
5. Garnish with sauce and serve warm.

Nutritional information

Calories 261, Total Fat: 9g, Saturated Fat: 7g, Total Carbs: 30g, Net Carbs: 28g, Protein: 15g, Sugar: 18g, Fiber: 2g, Sodium: 527, Potassium: 0mg

Ninja Foodi Air Fryer Cauliflower

There are definitely healthy snacks and side dishes that are full of flavor. You might be surprised to find out they are actually like veggies. Air fried cauliflower is a healthy and gluten-free snack or side dish with no oil required during cooking.

Prep time: 10 minutes, **Cook time**: 15 minutes, **Serves**: 5

Ingredients

1 cauliflower head, stem removed

3 tbsp olive oil, divided

1 tbsp minced garlic

½ tbsp garlic salt

⅛ tbsp pepper

¼ tbsp paprika

½ tbsp old bay seasoning

Preparation Method

1. Preheat the air fryer to 400 degrees for at least 5 minutes prior to cooking.
2. Cut the cauliflower into small florets on a chopping board and put them in a small bowl.
3. Pour 1 ½ teaspoon of olive oil on top of the florets and mix them well. Pour the remaining 1 ½ teaspoon of olive oil on the florets and rub it on every piece so that they are well coated.
4. Sprinkle the garlic, garlic salt, pepper, paprika, and old bay seasoning on the florets and mix them gently.
5. Place the cauliflower in the air fryer basket ensuring they don't overlap and cook for 15 minutes. After every 5 minutes, flip the florets gently so that all sides will turn crispy.
6. Serve the cauliflower with a dipping sauce. Enjoy.

Nutritional Information

Calories 106, Total Fat: 9g, Saturated Fat: 1g, Total Carbs: 6g, Net Carbs: 4g, Protein: 2g, Sugar: 2g, Fiber: 2g, Sodium: 733mg, Potassium 344g

Ninja Foodi French Fries

It is hard to think of a french fry as healthy, but air-fried french fry is far more healthy as they are made with significant less oil than the deep-fried one. The crispy texture is more important in the overall taste.

Prep time: 15 minutes, **Cook time:** 23 minutes, **Serves**: 6

Ingredients

5 potatoes russet, medium

3 tbsp olive oil

½ tbsp seasoned salt

Preparation Method

1. Wash the potatoes and dry then slice them into strips with the skins on.
2. Place the sliced tomatoes in a bowl and pour olive oil. Rub the oil over the potatoes.
3. Transfer the potatoes into air fryer basket and close the lid.
4. Press the crisp button and set the temperature to 390 degrees for 23 minutes ensuring you flip after every 7 minutes.
5. Transfer to a serving platter and salt the fries.
6. Serve and enjoy.

Nutritional Information

Calories 164, Total Fat: 7g, Saturated Fat: 1g, Total Carbs:22g, Net Carbs: 18g, Protein: 4g, Fiber: 4g, Sodium: 211mg, Potassium 733g

Ninja Foodi Zucchini Chips

Crunchy food without the need of artery-clogging oil has been a game-changer. Air fried zucchini is a healthier alternative that comes out just as crunchy as deep-fried without any oil. Best of all it is a low carb and low-calorie dish. It is perfect for anyone following the paleo diet and it is keto-friendly.

Prep time: 10 minutes, **Cook time:** 13 minutes, **Serves:** 6

Ingredients

1 whisked egg

¾ cup panko bread crumbs

1 tbsp old bay

1 tbsp garlic salt

2 medium zucchini, sliced into dials

Olive oil spray

Preparation Method

1. Preheat the air fryer to 350 degrees for at least 5 minutes prior to cooking.
2. Place the whisked egg on a plate.
3. Mix the panko bread crumbs, old bay, and garlic salt until well combined.
4. Dip the zucchini pieces into egg then coat with the bread crumb mixture one at a time. Spread them in a trivet avoiding overlapping.
5. Spray the zucchini pieces with olive oil and close the lid.
6. Press the crisp button and cook for 13 minutes ensuring you flip after every 10 minutes.
7. Transfer to a serving platter.
8. Serve while hot and enjoy.

Nutritional Information

Calories 41, Total Fat: 1g, Saturated Fat: 1g, Total Carbs: 6g, Net Carbs: 5g, Protein: 2g, Sugar: 1g, Fiber: 1g, Sodium: 453mg, Potassium 25g

Ninja Foodi Cabbage

Many people don't like eating cabbage. The use of pressure cooker and air fryer makes the cabbage edges crispy and makes it taste amazing. Moreso air frying is the best way you can use leftover cabbage head in your cupboard.

Prep time: 5 minutes, **Cook time**: 17 minutes, **Serves**: 4

Ingredients

1 cabbage, washed and cut into quarters

1 cup water

¾ tbsp old bay

1 tbsp garlic salt

Olive oil spray

Preparation Method

1. Place the cabbage into your Ninja Foodi air fryer basket.
2. Add water to the inner pot and put the basket inside the pot.
3. Set the pressure to high for 1 minutes then do a quick release.
4. Open the lid, remove the basket from the pot and drain all water.
5. Spray the basket with olive oil and sprinkle with old bay and garlic salt and put it back into the pot.
6. Close the air fryer lid and cook for 16 minutes at 400 degrees.
7. Serve and enjoy.

Nutritional Information

Calories 58, Total Fat: 1g, Saturated Fat: 1g, Total Carbs: 13g, Net Carbs: 7g, Protein: 3g, Sugar: 7g, Fiber: 6g, Sodium:625mg, Potassium 386g

Ninja Foodi Brussel Sprout

The Brussel sprouts are among the most powerful type of vegetable superfoods for they are packed with immunity-boosting vitamin C and cancer-fighting traits. Tender Brussels with a bit of crispy outside will make you love this understated vegetable. These Brussel sprouts come out of the air fryer in minutes.

Prep time: 10 minutes, **Cook time**: 15 minutes, **Serves**: 4

Ingredients

2 lb brussel sprout, sliced lengthwise

2 tbsp olive oil

1 ¼ tbsp garlic salt, divided

¼ tbsp chili powder

1 tbsp apple cider vinegar

1 fresh lemon, halved

1 ½ tbsp melted butter

⅛ tbsp pepper

1 tbsp dijon mustard

Preparation Method

1. Preheat the air fryer to 390 degrees for at least 5 minutes prior to cooking.
2. In a bowl add Brussel sprouts, olive oil, 1 teaspoon garlic salt, chili powder, and apple cider vinegar. Squeeze ½ lemon juice into the bowl.Toss the ingredients well.
3. Transfer the coated Brussel in the air fryer basket and close the lid.
4. Cook for 15 minutes flipping the Brussel pieces after every 5 minutes.
5. When Brussel are cooking, blend the butter, the remaining ¼ teaspoon garlic salt, pepper, the remaining ½ squeezed lemon juice, and dijon mustard in a bowl.
6. When brussel are done, toss them in the butter mixture. Serve and enjoy.

Nutritional Information

Calories 183, Total Fat: 11g, Saturated Fat: 3g, Total Carbs: 17g, Net Carbs: 10g, Protein: 6g, Sugar: 4g, Fiber: 7g, Sodium: 825mg, Potassium 698g

Ninja Foodi Sweet Potato

Sweet potatoes cooked to perfection in the air fryer is a side dish that takes very little effort to make yet yield amazing results. Air frying sweet potatoes create a crispy skin on the outside but tender and fluffy on the inside. You are unlikely to get them like this when you are baking in the oven.

Prep time: 5 minutes, **Cook time**: 35 minutes, **Serves**: 4

Ingredients

4 sweet potatoes, washed

1 ½ tbsp olive oil

½ tbsp salt for salty-sweet flavor

Preparation Method

1. Poke all-around each sweet potato with a fork.
2. Rub the outside of each sweet potato with olive oil using your hands.
3. Sprinkle the outside of each sweet potato with salt if you want a salty-sweet flavor.
4. Turn the metal rack of the Ninja Foodi upside down and place the sweet potatoes on top.
5. Cook for 35 minutes in the air fryer at 390 degrees.
6. Remove the sweet potatoes and slice them adding toppings such as butter.
7. Serve and enjoy.

Nutritional Information

Calories 158, Total Fat: 5g, Total Carbs: 26g, Net Carbs: 23g, Protein: 2g, Sugar: 5g, Fiber: 3g, Sodium: 362mg, Potassium 438g

Air-Fried Chickpeas

Air fryer chickpeas are crispy, distinct flavored and a crumbly snack that you will love. Cooking in an air fryer reduces the cook time to 15 minutes, and makes it even crunchier than when done in an oven. The amazing fact about this dish is that it is vegan and gluten-free making it a healthier meal.

Prep time: 5 minutes, **cook time**: 20 minutes; **Serves** 4

Ingredients

19 oz can chickpeas, rinsed and drained

1 tbsp olive oil

⅛ tbsp garlic powder

¼ tbsp onion powder

½ tbsp paprika

¼ tbsp cayenne

Salt and pepper to taste

Preparation Method

1. Mix together chickpeas, olive oil, garlic, onion, paprika, cayenne, salt and pepper in a bowl.
2. Preheat your air fryer to 390 ˙F/ 200 ˙C, add the chickpeas mixture in air fryer container and cook for 12-15 minutes, tossing ocassionaly.
3. Allow to cool and serve.

Nutritional information

Calories 242, Total Fat: 6g, Saturated Fat: 0g, Total Carbs: 36g, Net Carbs: 26g, Protein: 11g, Sugar: 6g, Fiber: 10g, Sodium: 9mg, Potassium: 391mg

Air-Fryer Spinach Artichoke Dip

It's correct. Not only is Air-fried Spinach Artichoke Dip uncomplicated and tasty, but it is just prepared in 15 minutes time. This vegan dip is what my folks and I prefer when looking for dips. For sure, once you familiarize yourself with this dip you cannot avoid it. It is simply the appetizer that is best for parties, holiday feasts and game day tables.

Prep time: 5 minutes, **cook time**: 20 minutes; **Serves 8**

Ingredients

1 tbsp cooking spray

3 cups spinach, fresh and chopped

8 oz cream cheese, softened

¼ cup sour cream

¼ cup mayonnaise

1 garlic clove, peeled and grated

½ tbsp garlic powder

½ tbsp Italian seasoning, dried

¼ cup tbsp onion powder

Salt and pepper to taste

½ cup artichoke hearts, chopped and marinated

2 cups mozzarella cheese, shredded

Preparation Method

1. Spray cooking oil on the skillet and heat over medium heat. Add spinach and fry for 5 minutes then drain the excess liquid.
2. In a medium bowl whisk together cream cheese, sour cream, mayonnaise, garlic, garlic powder, Italian season, onion powder, salt, and pepper.
3. Mix cooked spinach, sliced artichokes and 1 cup shredded mozzarella cheese in air fryer safe dish. Preheat your air fryer to 375 ·F, insert the dish and air fry for 5 minutes.
4. Top with the remaining mozzarella cheese. Air fry further for 4-6 minutes. Serve warm.

Nutritional information

Calories 299, Total Fat: 27g, Saturated Fat: 13g, Total Carbs: 4g, Net Carbs: 3g, Protein: 10g, Sugar: 2g, Fiber: 1g, Sodium: 470mg, Potassium: 0mg

Air-Fried Parmesan Mushrooms

Air-fried Parmesan Mushroom is a super easy and tasty side dish. The secret of this tasty and handsome looking mushroom is the combination of locally sourced ingredients. Air fryer mushrooms are like oven grilled mushrooms yet only take 15 minutes to cook! The mushrooms are so yummy and can be taken alongside any main dish of your choice.

Prep time: 5 minutes, **cook time**: 20 minutes; **Serves** 4

Ingredients

1 lb Cremini mushrooms, rinsed and chopped

2 tbsp olive oil

1 tbsp garlic powder

1 tbsp Italian seasoning, dried

Salt and pepper to taste

¼ cup parmesan cheese, shredded

Preparation Method

1. Coat mushrooms with olive, garlic powder, and Italian seasoning.
2. Preheat your air fryer to 370 °F, arrange coated mushrooms in air fryer basket and air fry for 13 minutes.
3. Toss the mushrooms, add salt, pepper and parmesan cheese then air fry for 2 minutes.
4. Serve warm.

Nutritional information

Calories 116, Total Fat: 8g, Saturated Fat: 2g, Total Carbs: 6g, Net Carbs: 5g, Protein: 5g, Sugar: 2g, Fiber: 1g, Sodium: 92mg, Potassium: 0mg

Air Fryer Baked Russet Potatoes

Air-fried Baked Potatoes are vegan-friendly paleo diet that you should be craving for. It is so easy to make and only takes 1 hour to cook! It is beautifully crispy on the outside and creamy to the core: just as tasty air-fried potato ought to be!

Prep time: 5 minutes, **Cook time:** 1 hour, **Serves** 2

Ingredients

2 large scrubbed russet potatoes

1 tbsp peanut oil

½ tbsp coarse sea salt

Preparation Method

1. Preheat your air fryer to 200∘C (400∘F)
2. Spray your potatoes with peanut oil then sprinkle them with salt.
3. Place your potatoes in the basket of the air fryer.
4. Cook for about 1 hour or until done (pierce with a fork to test when done).

Nutritional information

Calories 344, Total Fat: 7.1g, Saturated Fat: 1g, Total Carbs: 64.5g, Net Carbs: 56.4g, Protein: 7.5g, Sugar: 3g, Fiber: 8.1g, Sodium: 462mg

Air Fryer Spicy Green Beans

This flavor pairing was motivated by a prominent diet at a restaurant chain. The Spicy Green Bean dish is so quick and easy to cook in air fryer. This cooked dish has an addictive taste and sweet aroma that will leave you craving for more. Furthermore, It only takes 25 minutes to prepare!

Prep time 10 minutes, **Cook time:** 25 minutes, **Serves** 4

Ingredients

12 oz trimmed fresh green beans

½ tbsp red pepper flakes

1 clove minced garlic

1 tbsp soy sauce

1 tbsp rice wine vinegar

1 tbsp sesame oil

Preparation Method

1. Preheat your air fryer to 200°C or 400°F.
2. Place green beans in a bowl.
3. In another bowl whisk all other ingredients together then pour them over the beans.
4. Toss them to coat then wait for 5 minutes to marinate.
5. Divide the green beans into two and place one half in the basket of air fryer, then cook for 12 minutes.
6. Shake the basket after 6 minutes of cooking time.
7. Repeat the process with the remaining half of the green beans.
8. Serve warm and enjoy.

Nutritional information

Calories 59, Total Fat: 3.6g, Saturated Fat: 1g, Total Carbs: 6.6g, Net Carbs: 3.6g, Protein: 1.7g, Sugar: 1g, Fiber: 3g, Sodium: 80mg, Potassium 192mg

Air Fryer Roasted Okra

Air-fried Roasted Okra has an aromatic scent and flavorful taste that will take your lunch or dinner to the next level! This side dish is so simple and quick to cook in just 15 minutes! The dish is low in carbs and favorable for individuals thinking of consuming fewer calories!

Prep time: 5 minutes, **Cook time:** 15minutes, **Serves** 1

Ingredients

½ lb okra, pods sliced and ends trimmed,

¼ tbsp salt

1 tbsp olive oil

⅛ tbsp ground black pepper

Preparation Method

1. Preheat air fryer to 350∘F
2. Mix all ingredients in a bowl and gently stir.
3. Place in one layer in the air fryer basket.
4. Cook for 5minutes toss and cook for 5 more minutes, toss again and add 2 minutes of cooking.
5. Serve immediately.

Nutritional information

Calories 113, Total Fat: 5g, Saturated Fat: 1g, Total Carbs: 16.1g, Net Carbs: 8.8g, Protein: 4.6g, Sugar: 3g, Fiber: 7.3g, Sodium: 600mg, Potassium 691mg

Air Fryer Vegetable Kebabs

Vegetable kebabs are so easy and speedy to cook, in only 10 minutes. This vegan appetizer is a healthy low carb that weight watchers should prefer because the vegan skewers are gluten-free, paleo and low in calories. The air fryer vegetable kebab is also a flavorsome meal that will always leave you salivating for more bites!

Prep time: 10 minutes, cook time: 20 minutes; Serves 3

Ingredients

6-inch skewers

1 eggplant (Diced into 1-inch pieces)

1 zucchini (Diced into 1-inch pieces)

½ onion

Salt and pepper to taste

Preparation Method

1. If you intend to use wooden skewers, let them rest in a basin of water for 10 minutes prior to usage.
2. Thread the chopped veggies on the skewers and season with a little salt and pepper.
3. Preheat your air fryer to 390 ·F. Arrange skewers and air fry for about 10 minutes.
4. Serve warm.

Nutritional information

Calories 80, Total Fat: 0g, Saturated Fat: 0g, Total Carbs: 17g, Net Carbs: 10g, Protein: 3g, Sugar: 3g Fiber: 7g, Sodium: 12mg, Potassium: 714mg

Air Fryer Lemon Pepper Shrimp

I anticipate this stimulates you to read further, and perhaps entices you to dash to the kitchenette and cook the Air-fried Lemon Pepper Shrimp. Actually, the robust taste of this dish will make you enjoy your shrimp together with friends. The air fryer is easy and simple to make in just 10 minutes! The shrimp can be spooned out on top of rice or pasta or salad.

Prep time: 5 minutes, Cook time 10 minutes, Serves 2

Ingredients

1 tbsp olive oil

1 tbsp lemon pepper

1 lemon juiced

12 oz medium shrimp, uncooked peeled and deveined

¼ tbsp garlic powder

¼ tbsp paprika

1 sliced lemon

Preparation Method

1. Preheat your air fryer to 400°F
2. Mix together olive oil, lemon pepper, lemon juice, garlic powder and paprika in a medium bowl.
3. Add in shrimp then toss until coated.
4. Place shrimp in your air fryer then cook for 6-8 minutes or until firm and turns pink.
5. Serve immediately with lemon slices.

Nutritional information

Calories 215, Total Fat: 8.6g, Saturated Fat: 1.0g, Total Carbs: 12.6g, Net Carbs: 7.1g, Protein: 28.9g, Fiber: 5.5g, Sodium: 528mg, Potassium: 414mg

Air Fryer Soy-Ginger Shishito Peppers

The amazing part of Air-fried Ginger Shishito Peppers is that it features readily available ingredients. It is a palatable appetizer that is quick to make in just 10 minutes! It's an exceptional appetizer, mainly when coated with soy sauce, lime, honey, and ginger.

Prep time: 10 minutes, **Cook time** 10 minutes, **Serves** 4.

Ingredients

6 oz shishito peppers

1 tbsp vegetable oil

1 tbsp honey

1 tbsp fresh lime juice

½ tbsp fresh ginger, grated,

1 tbsp reduced-sodium soy sauce

Preparation Method

1. Preheat your air fryer to 390°F (199°C)
2. In a medium bowl toss peppers with vegetable oil to coat then place them in your air fryer basket.
3. Cook for 6 to 7 minutes shaking the basket when halfway through.
4. Meanwhile combine honey, lime juice, ginger, and soy sauce in a bowl then add the cooked peppers and toss to coat.
5. Serve warm and enjoy.

Nutritional information

Calories 36, Total Fat: 1.2g, Total Carbs: 6.2g, Net Carbs: 6.2g, Protein: 1.1g, Sugar: 4g, Fiber: 0.7g, Sodium: 136mg, Potassium: 156mg

Ninja Foodi Buffalo Cauliflower Bites

These crispy air fryer Buffalo cauliflower bites are the perfect appetizer. You might even forget that they are vegetarian because the coating and the sauce is the perfect combo. They come together in no time without having to dredge in flour.

Prep time: 5 minutes, **Cook time**: 20 minutes, **Serves**: 4

Ingredients

½ bag cauliflower florets, frozen

Olive oil spray

1 cup hot sauce, divided

¾ cup panko breadcrumbs

Preparation Method

1. Place the cauliflower in a bowl and spray them with olive oil then toss.
2. Pour ½ cup of hot sauce over cauliflower and toss until well coated.
3. Pour the panko bread crumbs over the cauliflower and toss well.
4. Place the cauliflower in the air fryer and cook for 20 minutes at 205 degrees ensuring you toss after every 5 minutes.
5. Transfer to a serving platter and drizzle the remaining ½ cup of hot sauce over the cauliflower bites.
6. Serve and enjoy.

Nutritional Information

Calories 31, Total Fat: 1g, Total Carbs: 3g, Net Carbs: 1g, Protein: 4g, Sugar: 1g, Fiber: 2g, Sodium: 920mg, Potassium 165g

Ninja Foodi Cheesy Garlic Bread

Perfectly crunchy garlic bread with cheese can be on your table in just 8 minutes thanks to air fryer cooking. The cheesy garlic bread is made crispy on the outside and chewy in the middle. Butter, garlic, and mozzarella cheese on the crusty bread is toasted to perfection in the air fryer.

Prep time: 8 minutes, **Cook time**: 8 minutes, **Serves**: 3

Ingredients

3 slices crusty french bread

2 tbsp butter, softened

½ tbsp garlic powder

½ cup mozzarella cheese

Preparation Method

1. Apply butter to the bread then sprinkle it with garlic powder.
2. Place the rack of the Foodi on the lowest setting in the pot and place bread on it.
3. Sprinkle the bread with cheese and air fry for 8 minutes at 360 degrees.
4. Serve and enjoy.

Nutritional Information

 Calories 310, Total Fat: 13g, Saturated Fat: 8g, Total Carbs: 37g, Net Carbs: 35g, Protein: 12g, Sugar: 2g, Fiber: 2g, Sodium: 512mg, Potassium 96g

CONCLUSION

There you have it, a compilation of 100 delicious recipes to make in your Ninja Foodi Digital Airfryer. We've also given you a 28 day meal plan to help transition to making delicious meals with your airfryer. Our goal is to make life using the new cooking appliance as easy as possible. We hope by following our recipes you'll live a healthy life and sidestep the serious consequences of consuming too much cholesterol.

CPSIA information can be obtained
at www.ICGtesting.com
Printed in the USA
BVHW091053181121
621929BV00010B/213